HEATING WITH WOOD

HEATING WITH WOOD

By the Editors of
THE FAMILY HANDYMAN Magazine

Butterick Publishing

Photographs and Illustrations: Bark Buster, Better Way Products, Gary
Branson, Ron Bruzek, Ron Chamberlain, Den Mar Corp., Double Star,
Duo-Matic, Energy Tightwad, Fortier Energy, Hearth Craft, Heatilator,
Homelite—Div. of Textron, Kristia Assoc., Locke Stove Co., Martic
Industries, McCulloch, Bill Minnehan, Jim Morris, Pioneer Lamps and
Stoves, Preway, Pro-Sharp Corporation, Chuck Redlin, Gene Schnaser,
Southport Stove, True Temper, U.S. Stove Co., Washington Stove Works,
Wilson Ind., Z-Brick.

Book Design: Remo Cosentino

Copyright © 1978 by Butterick Publishing
                    708 Third Avenue
                    New York, New York 10017
                    A Division of American Can Company

Manufactured and printed in the United States of America, published
simultaneously in the USA and Canada.

Library of Congress Cataloging in Publication Data
Main entry under title:

Heating with wood.

  Includes index.
  1. Heating. 2. Wood as fuel. 3. Stoves, Wood. 4. Fireplaces. I. The
Family Handyman.
TH7437.H43   697'.04   78-16113
ISBN 0-88421-077-4

Acknowledgements

This book on heating with wood exists because of the cooperation and assistance of a long list of manufacturers, agencies, associations, and authors. I especially wish to thank Paul Stegmeir, forester and wood-heating specialist, and Gene Schnaser, editor of THE FAMILY HANDYMAN Magazine, for advice and guidance throughout the preparation of the manuscript. This book also would not have been possible without the assistance of the editors of Wood Burning Quarterly, Yankee Magazine, and the contributions of the following authors: Bill Minnehan, Gary Branson, A. J. Hand, Lars Nelson, Lorn Manthey, Jim Morris, Clyde Hunt, Linwood B. Rideout, Tom Neff, and Richard Jagels. Also a special thanks to Paula Smith, Dawn Johnson, and Betty Helsper for their help in shaping the manuscript into its final form.

Howard Jones, Publisher
THE FAMILY HANDYMAN Magazine

Contents

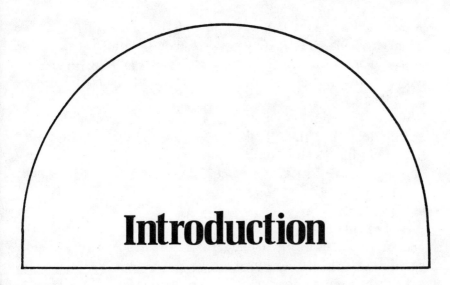

Introduction

Today, after decades of wasteful use of fossil fuels, energy reserves have fallen to a crisis level. At government urging, many dollars are being spent to develop alternative sources of energy. The search, however, has involved more than looking for ways to harness the sun, wind, water, and even garbage. It has also led to a rediscovery of what our forebears knew as a matter of fact:

Nature stores massive amounts of energy every year in the form of wood.

Our ancestors, viewing the sweeping forests of this continent, found woodland and forest riches beyond belief. Demands of a growing nation, however, led to massive assaults upon the virgin forests which had been thousands of years in the making. Total acreage of U.S. forests fell from 2 billion acres to 800 million acres by 1900.

World War I put massive demands upon our remaining forests, and by 1920 forest fires were claiming 30 to 40 million acres annually. Fortunately, through fire control and careful cutting and restocking of trees, our forest reserves have been rebuilt back to 765 million acres.

Little of this wood is being used to heat the homes of

America. Back in 1950, only 20% of the homes in the U.S. burned wood—mostly from waste wood, small farm wood lots and the like. As recently as 1970 only 6% of the wood harvested was used for fuel; most wood cut is used for other purposes.

Wood for home heating is reasonably accessible and economical as a fuel. The energy available is tremendous. Seasoned hardwood, such as oak, beech, and hickory, has about half the Btu value of coal. A cord of wood (a stack 4′ x 4′ x 8′) weighs 2 tons. Its heat value is equal to 1 ton of anthracite coal.

As the cost of gas, oil, and electric energy rises, wood will become even more of a bargain. In most areas fossil fuel costs are rising 10% or more per year. The cost of these fuels may soon become academic. Known reserves of fossil fuels are estimated to be only a 15-year supply.

Wood does have several drawbacks to a society used to automation. It is bulky, requires labor to cut, takes up storage room, and, when burned, demands more attention than fossil fuel heat systems. From an ecological standpoint, however, wood is not only a renewable resource, it also pollutes the air less than fossil fuels.

This book was written to help you learn or relearn the techniques of using wood for heat. It combines woodburning lore of the past with the technology of today. By studying the following pages you'll learn how to use the renewable energy of wood in your own home—wisely, efficiently, and safely.

The Editors of
THE FAMILY HANDYMAN Magazine

1
How
To Get
Firewood

In almost every part of the country, with the exception of large metropolitan areas and deserts, you should be able to find an inexpensive source of firewood even if you don't own a tree.

Start looking well before the burning season, since wood needs time to dry before burning. Ask your friends, relatives, or neighbors if you can have their dead or diseased trees. Often they'll let you have some free if you help them gather their own personal firewood.

FINDING WOOD

Dumps and landfills are filled with hundreds of cords of discarded wood each year because local ordinances don't allow open burning. Usually you are welcome to take whatever you want.

State forests and parks will sometimes allow the removal of designated trees for private woodburning. A permit may be required. Your local county agent, park manager, or state Department of Forestry or Department of Natural Resources will fill you in on the details in your area. The same goes for national forests.

Utility companies routinely remove trees and branches

from their rights of way. Generally anyone can have the wood unless it is on private property. Sawmills are a source of wood that shouldn't be overlooked. Some will sell the slabs, but others are glad when you ask to take it.

Construction crews for roads, industrial sites, and new home developments must remove some of the trees on a site. They often bury trees unless somebody goes in and asks for the wood.

In rural areas you can—and should—get permission from landowners to clean up wooded areas. Particularly good sites to ask about are the trees along creeks or a wooded area some distance from the dwelling. By simply removing fallen trees in a single grove you can get enough firewood to burn a full season. An advantage is that since the trees have already fallen, you won't have to wait for the wood to dry.

CUTTING YOUR OWN

Your own yard trees can provide some wood. Utilize prunings and dead or diseased trees. Don't overlook the value of wood from either your own fruit trees or those of neighboring orchards. Most orchard owners, however, realize the value of their wood and cut and sell it themselves. Fruitwood is some of the best wood available and gives off a fragrant aroma when burned.

If you are lucky enough to have your own wood lot, cleaning up dead wood is an obvious source of firewood. Dead limbs and dying stems that would only rot may provide all the fuel needed for occasional fires. Such scavenging, however, only skims the surface. Careful management will improve your wood lot and often yield a cord per acre annually.

The renewed use of wood for fuel creates an opportunity to correct mistakes in wood lots that have been mismanaged, overcut, or just neglected. Chances are good that many wood lots have been left with an overabundance of crooked, diseased, and otherwise unsalable trees. These hamper the growth of the more desirable straight and healthy trees that are valuable for lumber and veneer.

Thinning Stands

To get wood to burn and improve a wood lot, first remove less desirable trees, especially those that compete with the best crop trees. Trees need room to grow at their maximum rates. If too close together, they compete for water, nutrients, and sunlight, and grow more slowly. A young stand of trees starts with 1,000 to 6,000 stems per acre. At maturity, when they measure about 20" in diameter, less than 100 trees per acre will survive. Most of the young trees die before they are large enough to harvest for saw logs.

This is a natural selection process and it is slow, requiring 150 to 200 years or more to complete. Thinning hardwood stands when they are young hastens the process by permitting the more desirable trees to grow rapidly throughout their lives. Removing competing trees by frequent thinnings enables the stand to produce larger, higher-quality trees. This promotes a greater volume of wood per acre in a reduced period of time—much less than 100 years. Before thinning your hardwood stand, know the value of the trees you are thinning. Check with your local forester for advice and hints on tree identification.

Begin by thinning as early as possible to gain the benefits of repeated thinnings. Saplings between 1" and 4" in diameter at breast height (about 4½' aboveground) are easiest to weed out. The remaining saplings will respond most rapidly to reduced competition. Unfortunately, your woodpile grows rather slowly when you work with this size tree. You may have to cut 100 or more saplings before you have a cord of firewood. Such small sticks are little more than kindling wood. While some kindling wood is always welcome, cutting and stacking it can be disappointingly slow.

Progress in adding to your woodpile can proceed more rapidly when you thin in stands that average 4" to 10" in diameter. Trees of this size are commonly referred to as poles. They may be used for pulpwood, fence posts, or fuelwood. Thinning encourages increased growth of the remaining stems, and avoids that normal stagnant period of slow diameter-growth in tight pole stands.

Before doing anything in larger wood lot areas, get technical advice from your local publicly employed service forester. He can advise you of the potential value of your trees and which young, high-quality stems should be retained to increase in growth and value.

Selecting Crop Trees

The best way to thin a young pole stand is the crop tree selection method. This is a simple method for thinning stands to the greatest advantage of the best trees in the stand. Cut competing trees for firewood.

The trees selected as crop trees should be straight and tall with relatively small branches and should show signs of self-pruning: the lower 10′ to 16′ of the tree should have few or no branches. A few small dead branches in this section are a good indication that the tree will develop into a good-quality tree, free of defects. Trees with swollen stems, broken or seamed bark, mechanical wounds, and poorly healed branch stubs are best removed and used for firewood.

Look up into the crown. The crown of a crop tree needs 3′ to 4′ of open space on at least two sides. Those trees touching the crown of your crop tree are the competitors. They may be removed for firewood. In most cases, removing one or two side competitors will provide the crop tree with the space it needs, but don't hesitate to remove more if necessary.

One good way to thin crop trees is this: Start 10′ to 20′ into the stand or from the property line. Select a crop tree and identify it, either by tying a ribbon around it at breast height, or by using a spot of paint. Then, pace about 20′ (eight steps) on a line parallel to the edge of the stand or property line. Mark the closest crop tree within a 5′ to 7′ radius. If there are no trees that meet crop tree specifications within this circle, pick out the best of the lot and mark it. If there are no trees, pace out another 5′ (two steps) and try again. If there aren't any trees within 7′ of the second spot, skip it and start over again at the next spot 20′ away.

COMPARISON OF ENERGY SOURCES FOR HEATING

Fuel	Unit	Heating Efficiency	Heating Values 1000's of Btu's Per Unit[4]		Units Needed to Give 1,000,000 Btu's of Available Heat
			Total	Available[4]	
Natural Gas	mcf[1]	70%	1,000	700	1.43[4]
#1 Fuel Oil (Kerosene)	gallon	65%	135	87.8	11.4
#2 Fuel Oil	gallon	65%	141	91.7	10.9
Propane	gallon	70%	91	63.7	15.7
Electricity	kwh	100%	3.413	3.413	293
Coal					
Anthracite	ton	60%	25,400	15,240	0.066
High-Volatile Bituminous C	ton	60%	22,000	13,200	0.076
Low-Volatile Bituminous C	ton	60%	28,600	17,160	0.058
Lignite	ton	60%	13,800	8,280	0.12
Charcoal	pound	60%	13	7.8	128
Wood					
Aspen	cord[2]	50%	14,700[3]	7,300	0.137
Jack Pine	cord	50%	17,100	8,500	0.118
Paper Birch	cord	50%	20,300	10,200	0.098
White Oak	cord	50%	25,700	12,800	0.078

Source: University of Minnesota

[1] 1,000 Cubic Feet
[2] 128 Cubic Feet
[3] Assuming 85 Cubic Feet Of Solid Wood Per Cord At 20% Moisture Content.
[4] For Other Efficiencies: AVAILABLE HEAT = TOTAL HEAT x EFFICIENCY
UNITS NEEDED = 1,000,000 ÷ AVAILABLE HEAT.

Follow this procedure until you reach the far edge of your stand or the distance you have previously decided to go into the stand. When you reach the end of the first line, pace off 20′ at a right angle to the first line. Pick a crop tree, mark it, then go back along a line parallel to the first line. Use the paint spots or ribbons on the crop trees of the first line to guide you as you proceed on the second line.

Ideally, pick a crop tree every 20′ and release its crown. As nature doesn't space trees evenly, it is impossible to adhere rigidly to this distance. But by using it as a guide you will end up with a sufficient number of released trees (about 100 per acre). As you walk through your stand, don't hesitate to pick a good crop tree even though it is growing within 15′ of the last one. If it is impossible to locate an ideal crop tree within 25′, pick the best one you have.

This is a slow procedure at first. But as you gain experience and confidence in yourself, the work will progress faster and be more enjoyable.

Harvesting Trees

After you have selected the crop trees for release, you can begin harvesting your stand. First, remove trees that touch or are too close to the crown of the crop trees. They are direct competitors. Allow 3′ to 4′ between crowns on at least two sides.

In some high-quality stands, the trees to be removed are as high in quality as the crop tree. Although this may be disturbing, remember that most of the trees you are removing will not live to maturity. At some future time, they will be shaded out and die. Furthermore, the crop trees you release will grow faster so they will regain some of the growth you lose by removing the competition.

Sometimes a compromise is in order. If two high-quality trees are side by side, the best decision might be to accept both as crop trees and to release each on two sides.

In most pole stands, there is an abundance of "understory" trees that are much smaller than the crop trees. Their crowns are seen below the crowns of the larger trees. In

CHARACTERISTICS OF FIREWOOD

Wood	Wet Medium Dry	Sparks	Amount of Smoke	Ease of Splitting
Hickory	Medium	Some	Little	Well
Red Oak	Wet	Few	Little	Well
White Oak	Wet	Few	Little	Well
Sugar Maple	Medium	Few	Moderate	Fair
Red Maple	Wet	Few	Moderate	Fair
Beech	Dry	Few	Little	Hard
Ash	Dry	Few	Little	Well
White Birch	Wet	Some	Little	Easy
Yellow Birch	Medium	Some	Moderate	Hard
Cottonwood (Poplar)	Very Wet	Few	Moderate	Hard
Sycamore Willow	Very Wet	Many	Lots	Hard
Elm	Wet	Few	Moderate	Extremely Hard
Pine, white or yellow	Dry	Moderate	Lots	Well
Cedar	Dry	Many	Moderate	Easy
Fir	Dry	Many	Moderate	Easy
Redwood	Dry	Moderate	Moderate	Fair

such a position, they are deprived of sunlight—nature's way of removing them from the stand. Harvest any understory trees big enough for firewood. Their removal will have little effect on the growth of the crop trees, but they will provide enough firewood to make the effort worthwhile.

After releasing the crop trees, your next concern is the dead, dying, and deformed trees that hinder the development of the area. Any of these trees that have not been removed in thinning could also be harvested for firewood.

Note: More important than anything else is your own safety. Felling trees and trimming branches of any kind presents potentially serious hazards. Work with an experienced woodsman, if possible, before attempting woodcutting yourself. Exercise caution at all times, and be certain

Felling a Tree

First decide on your retreat. When the tree starts to fall, make your first horizontal cut one third of the way through. Make another cut down at an angle to notch the tree in the direction you want it to fall. *Caution:* The tree can now fall at any time.

This is how the tree should look with the notch removed. Save the notches—they make good, long-lasting firewood.

Make the back cut 2" above the point of the notch, leaving at least 2" for a hinge.

Notice how the wood acts as a hinge while the tree is falling. The hinge will break as the tree falls.

Start at the top of the tree to remove the limbs. Be careful as you get to the base or to heavier branches—some of these branches may be holding tons of force just waiting to be released. Cut as many branches as possible before tangling with the ones supporting the tree. When these are cut the tree may roll. If the tree is on a hill, stand on the uphill side of the branch being cut. If branches have pressure on them, cut one third of the way through from the top. Then make an undercut partway through, get away, and let the tree finish the job. See Chapter 3 for helpful tips on felling trees and safety precautions.

you have studied your chain saw operator's manual for safety rules. Stay alert at all times while working in the woods. Check other chapters in this book for pointers on how to keep woodcutting a safe, accident-free activity.

Special Considerations

As you become better acquainted with your wood lot, you'll be increasingly aware of its wildlife. Careful use of the chain saw will provide them with more food by allowing a more lush growth of forage close to the ground. Some compromise may be necessary to retain an old, valuable oak that regularly produces large crops of acorns. Save a den tree—it's easier on the animals if you choose another tree to burn, rather than their home.

Small clearings and patch cuttings where cull trees stand also help provide the interspersed feed and cover needed by wildlife. As small openings are made, you can promote seed production, stimulate young, vigorous growth on the forest floor, and provide yourself with logs that bring back the glow of summer suns of long ago.

BUYING FIREWOOD

When buying firewood, remember there is very little difference in the heat values of a pound of various woods. The difference is in the pounds of wood per cord, and the burning characteristics of that wood.

Since price usually is determined by the cord—a measure of volume, not weight—the amount of heat available in a cord depends on the type of wood. Due to countless natural variables inherent in wood, scaling (the art of measuring cut wood) is not an exact science.

Often, a cord of wood is defined simply as a pile 8' long, 4' high, and 4' wide. These dimensions are for what is recognized as a "standard cord." However, a cord can be just about any set of dimensions as long as both parties to the trade understand and are in agreement.

There are several reasons for the development of the 8'x 4'x 4' size. In the woods, a piece 4' long is about the

A cord of wood is 8' long, 4' wide, and 4' high, or any combination of measurements that produces 128 cubic feet. A fireplace cord contains one-third as much wood. A face cord is any stack of wood 8' long and 4' high that is cut to burning lengths of 12", 16", 20", or 24".

maximum that can be handled by one person. A 4' unit rides well crosswise on most rigs used to haul wood. And when the 4' length is fitted for a stove, the multiples of two 24" or three 16" or four 12" are convenient to saw and "fit up even," as the saying goes. The 4' height of the pile is about as high as can be easily hand lifted, and it is not readily tipped over. The 8' length of a pile divides evenly into fractions of a cord—2' for a quarter cord, 4' for a half cord.

COMPARISON OF HEATING VALU

Species	Average Specific Gravity at 20% Moisture Content	Density of Wood at 20% Moisture Content[1] (pounds/cubic feet)	Average Wei of 85 Cubic F of Wood at 2 Moisture Con (pounds)
Hickory (Avg. of Several Types)	.68	50.9	4,327
Eastern Hophornbeam	.67	50.2	4,267
Apple	.65	48.7	4,140
White Oak	.63	47.2	4,012
Sugar Maple	.59	44.2	3,757
Red Oak	.59	44.2	3,757
Beech	.59	44.2	3,757
Yellow Birch	.58	43.4	3,689
White Ash	.58	43.4	3,689
Hackberry	.51	38.2	3,247
Tamarack	.51	38.2	3,247
Paper Birch	.50	37.4	3,179
Cherry	.49	36.7	3,120
Elm (White or American)	.48	35.9	3,052
Black Ash	.47	35.2	2,992
Red Maple (Soft Maple)	.46	34.4	2,924
Boxelder	.44	32.9	2,797
Jack Pine	.42	31.4	2,669
Norway Pine	.42	31.4	2,669
Hemlock	.39	29.2	2,482
Black Spruce	.39	29.2	2,482
Aspen	.36	27.0	2,295
White Pine	.35	26.3	2,236
Balsam Fir	.35	26.3	2,236
Cottonwood	.33	24.8	2,108
Basswood	.33	24.8	2,108
N. White Cedar	.30	22.5	1,913

[1]Density = weight and volume at 20% moisture content.
[2]Conversion Factors: at 20% moisture content, there are approximately 6,400 Btu's per pound of v

R SEVERAL SPECIES OF WOOD

Possible Recoverable Heat Units Per Cord of 85 Solid Cubic Feet and Assuming 100% Efficiency[2] (in millions of Btu's) 20% Moisture Content	Available Heat Per Cord at 50% Heating Efficiency (in millions of Btu's)	Units Needed to Give 1,000,000 Btu's of Available Heat (cords)
27.7	13.8	.072
27.3	13.7	.073
26.5	13.2	.076
25.7	12.8	.078
24.0	12.0	.083
24.0	12.0	.083
24.0	12.0	.083
23.6	11.8	.085
23.6	11.8	.085
20.8	10.4	.096
20.8	10.4	.096
20.3	10.2	.098
20.0	10.0	.100
19.5	9.8	.102
19.1	9.6	.104
18.7	9.4	.106
17.9	8.9	.112
17.1	8.5	.118
17.1	8.5	.118
15.9	7.9	.127
15.9	7.9	.127
14.7	7.3	.137
14.3	7.2	.139
14.3	7.2	.139
13.5	6.7	.149
13.5	6.7	.149
12.2	6.1	.164

Source: University of Minnesota

When someone with hand tools fells limbs, junks, splits, and stacks a pile 8′ x 4′ x 4′ in a day, it is a traditional symbol of an honest day's work. In the past, an 8′ x 4′ x 4′ pile of firewood hauled out of the woods on one load signified a good team of horses and good scouting. Old-timers who had an 8′ x 4′ x 4′ cord of seasoned hardwood in the shed felt assured that their woodburning kitchen stove was taken care of for the coldest months of January and February.

The outside measurements of a stocked pile of 4′ wood can be accurately expressed in terms of cords and fractions. But it is also of great importance in the fair determination of a cord that conditions other than these outside dimensions be considered.

By nature, some logs have warts and big washer knots on the sides, so they are not really round. Most logs have a taper of some degree. Others have unsound wood caused by rot. In addition, stacking of a cord can affect its dimensions. All of the big ends may be piled on the face so that the front of the pile appears higher than the back. The pile may be set over a stump or rock. It may be piled crisscross. Logs may be sawed off to something other than 48″ long. Long knots may be left so that the wood will not lie together properly. These are the sort of conditions that are difficult to identify and list. On-the-spot reasonable judgment is the best answer.

A standard cord of 8′ x 4′ x 4′ occupies a space of 128 cubic feet. This 128 cubic feet of space, in any combination of heights and lengths (providing the pieces are 4′ long), is still a standard cord. But an average cord of wood, piled in a reasonable manner, has been found to contain between 80 and 90 cubic feet of solid wood; the rest is empty space, due to the uneven shape of cut wood.

You can help make sure you receive a reasonable solid wood content by checking to see if it has been piled in a way that allows accurate measuring of the height and length. Check the length of several pieces of wood to see how close they measure to 48″ long. One inch short on the average means nearly a 2% loss in solid wood content; 6″ short, nearly 12%. Short wood is the buyer's loss, and wood longer than 48″, the buyer's gain. Measure the average height of both front and back sides of the pile.

Other considerations: Watch out for wood that is so rotten it never will burn. Make sure the species is what the seller says it is. Remember that when you buy 4′ of wood, it must be sawed to length and, in some cases, split before it can be used in a conventional stove.

2

How
To Use
Saws And Axes

There are many ways to cut wood and tools to use to get the job done safely and quickly. Whether you use a manual saw or a chain saw, don't go out alone. Bring a friend along to make the job easier and more enjoyable. And if an accident should happen, you'll have help right there.

Wear snug-fitting clothes that don't restrict your movement or get caught on limbs and brush. If you don't have them, it would be wise to invest in a good pair of steel-toed boots which support the ankles well. A hard hat, goggles, and ear protection, along with chaps to protect the legs are also recommended accessories. Before you head for the woods, have the proper tools in good operating condition and know how to use them safely.

WOOD SAWS

With the rapid development of the chain saw during the past decade or two, the traditional saws that harvested timber and firewood for generations are often relegated to dusty corners of woodsheds and secondhand shops. These castoff saws, once the cherished tools for a multitude of cutting chores, are still valuable for the wood user.

With a little searching, a good timber saw can be purchased almost anywhere. Two-man and one-man timber saws, as well as numerous bucksaws, appear regularly at country auctions, usually for less than $10. Browsing through secondhand stores and antique shops will often produce saws as well. Local hardware stores often carry various pruning saws and metal-framed bow saws.

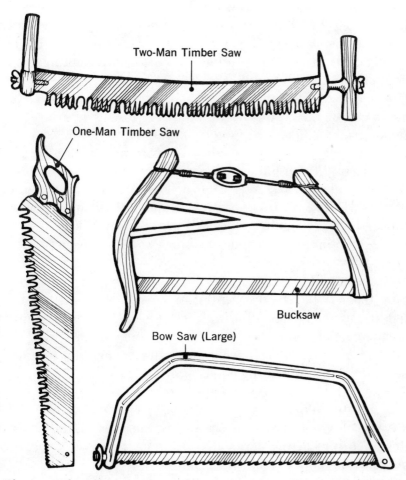

The saws for the manual woodcutter: two-man timber saw, one-man timber saw, bucksaw, and bow saw.

The large bow saws are excellent, but avoid the small ones which are good only for limbing operations. Traditional timber saws and bucksaws are still manufactured, but usually have to be ordered by mail and prices are quite high. This is offset, however, by the high quality of these saws, which should last a lifetime.

While looking for old saws, you are bound to run into the venerable cordwood or circular cutoff saw. Farmers have traditionally considered this to be the fastest saw for reducing pole-size logs to firewood bolts. This saw is typically powered by a tractor, but if you should find a small one in good shape and can rig it to an electric motor, it will be handy and reasonably quiet for cutting up saplings and branchwood.

A word of caution: Even in good operating shape, these saws can be hazardous. After 20 to 50 years of deterioration in a farmer's field, the potential for malfunction is much greater. Get professional advice before purchasing or setting one up, if you have not worked with these saws before.

If you find an old saw that strikes your fancy, the next step is putting it into operating shape. Saw fitting involves more than just sharpening. All wood-cutting saws—two-man, one-man, straight, or circular—can have either crosscut or rip cutting teeth.

If the cutting teeth, viewed from the side of the saw, look like tepees that have been tilted to one side so that the leading edge is vertical or undercut, then you probably have a ripsaw. The way the teeth are sharpened provides the critical distinction. Crosscut teeth are beveled on the outside, leading and trailing edges to provide a knifelike cutting stroke. Rip teeth are not beveled, and the leading point looks like a tiny chisel. In fact, the ripsaw cuts by chipping off slivers of wood. Crosscut saws, as the name implies, are designed for cutting across the grain of the wood. Ripsaws cut parallel to the grain. For felling trees and cutting firewood, the crosscut saw is the one you want.

Some crosscut timber saws have additional teeth interspersed among the cutting teeth. These are called rakers.

Lance Tooth Pattern

Crosscut Teeth

Ripsaw Teeth

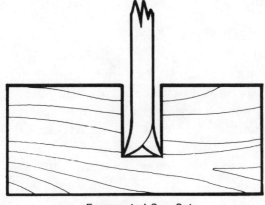

Exaggerated Saw Set

All saws fall into one of two categories: crosscut or ripsaws. For woodcutting you need a crosscut saw.

They help remove the chips from the saw kerf. Some saws may also have deep gullets between the teeth which serve the same purpose. Properly functioning rakers and gullets keep the saw from binding.

The cutting edge of most timber saws is slightly arched or curved, so that only a few teeth contact the wood at any time. This allows for a more effortless cutting action. Bucksaws and bow saws must be used with a rocking motion while cutting to achieve the same effect. One-man timber saws generally have a thicker blade to prevent buckling on the push stroke (two-man saws are always pulled). In addition to a thinner blade, two-man saws sometimes have a concave, arched back. This permits a wedge to be driven into the cut if binding occurs. All two-man saws have removable handles (the handles should never be permanently riveted) so the saw can be removed from a cut after a wedge is driven behind it.

Fitting Your Saw
To fit your saw, first check for broken teeth. Broken teeth will cause the saw to catch, perhaps snapping the blade, and possibly injuring you. If there are several broken teeth, the saw must be ground down to the lowest broken tooth, and all new teeth must be fashioned, using the stubs of the old ones as guides. Unless you have unlimited free time, hang the saw over your mantel (or even throw it out) and buy another. If the saw has no broken teeth, remove any rust. Surface rust can be removed with a chemical rust remover, fine steel wool and kerosene, or the traditional method—a chunk of pumice stone and water. Do not use a coarse abrasive as it will leave small gouges which can cause the saw to bind. After the saw is cleaned and wiped dry, it is ready for jointing.

Through the years, as a saw is repeatedly sharpened, some teeth become sharpened more than others. You can check this by placing a straight edge on the cutting edge—often, some teeth will not touch it. Those teeth, no matter how sharp, do no cutting. You can correct this by jointing. Joint a straight blade by placing it in a jig or other vise that has wooden jaws to protect the surface. Then hold the blade with the teeth facing upward and run a flat file over the teeth until all teeth are the same height. A "saw-jointer" or homemade jig will help hold the file perpendicular to the blade and keep you from scuffing all the skin off your fingers.

An additional step is required for a timber saw because of the rakers. If you plan to cut mostly hardwoods, the rakers should be filed down 1/64" to 1/40" below the cutting teeth. For softwoods, the raker-to-cutting clearance should be between 1/40" and 1/32". A commercially available fitting tool will accomplish the two tasks of jointing and raker filing on timber saws.

Jointing a circular saw—more precisely called truing—is a bit more difficult. A good approximation can be achieved by mounting the blade on the mandrel (axle) and rotating it backward by hand while holding a file or hand sharpening stone squarely across the teeth. More accurate truing can be achieved by building a jig that will hold the blade horizontally. You then rotate the blade while feeding it into a motorized grinding wheel.

Once the saw is jointed or trued, it should be gummed—a process of deepening the gullets between the teeth. On carpenter saws and some bucksaws and timber saws, the bases of the teeth meet at an acute angle. These saws are gummed with a taper (triangular) file. Many timber saws and bucksaws have rounded gullets between at least some of the teeth. A round file of the appropriate diameter can be used, but a gumming wheel on a motorized grinder is faster.

Gumming wheels come in various widths, so check the gullets on your saw before purchasing one. The amount of gumming required can be estimated on a straight saw by examining the teeth near a handle—these teeth generally show little wear. If you can find a new saw or one in good condition that is similar to yours, this will be even more useful for comparison. If the saw binds too much, then gumming or setting is needed.

Setting generally follows jointing and gumming. If the saw teeth are not alternately bent to either side of the blade, the kerf becomes so narrow the blade will bind. The saw teeth are bent to either side so that the cutting edge of the saw is thicker than the blade itself. The cut, or kerf, in the wood will then be wider than the blade, and the blade will not bind in the wood. The amount of set depends on the design of the teeth and the kind of wood to be cut. Soft or wet wood requires greater saw set than hard or dry wood. Rakers, if present, are not set. (If the teeth on your saw are extremely worn, the saw may have to be sharpened prior to setting, and then touched up again.)

Setting can be done with either a hammer and setting block, or a hand-operated spring set. The spring set is more accurate and easier to use. If the set of the teeth seems to be uniform and the saw does not bind, you can postpone setting until a later fitting.

Your saw is now ready for sharpening. Not all the previous steps are necessary each time the saw is sharpened, but they ought to be checked periodically.

Sharpening techniques differ somewhat depending on the saw type. Small ripsaws can easily be sharpened with a taper file. In this case, the front edge of the tooth is filed perpendicular and the trailing edge is automatically set at 30°. The file is stroked squarely across the blade, producing a chiseled edge with no side bevel.

In sharpening a crosscut saw, you can use either a taper file or, for larger saws, a flat file. Try to maintain the same bevels and angles (on a straight saw the teeth near a handle are often the best models). Teeth are alternately sharpened on opposite sides—the beveled surfaces facing the direction of the tooth set.

Once the bevels come to a point, do not file any further or the saw will have to be jointed again. On a timber saw with raker teeth, the rakers are filed from the inside of the arch until a chiseled edge is achieved. Further filing will change the clearance between rakers and cutting teeth, so stop filing as soon as the chiseled edge is achieved. Once the saw is fitted, coat the blade with a light oil to prevent rust.

WOOD AXES

To most modern woodchoppers, all axes are created equal, and buying a new axe is as simple as walking into the local hardware store and picking one off the rack. At the turn of the century, when axe technology crested, a comparison of the favorite axe of several dozen woodsmen might have revealed as many varieties of axes as woodsmen. Personal preferences and local wood conditions encouraged the evolution of hundreds of combinations of axe shapes, weights, and handle lengths and designs. Regional axe standards ranged from the 2½- to 4-pound single-bit axe on 28″- to 32″-long handles in New England, up to hefty 7-pound Bunyan-style double-bit axes with 48″ handles adapted for use in the big timber country of the Far West.

Before the introduction of machines capable of mass-producing axe handles, axe heads came without the handle attached. Even after the Civil War, when axes with factory-attached handles became available, exacting woodsmen still preferred to attach a carefully handcrafted handle to a favorite axe according to his particular specifications. After fitting axe to handle, the woodsman would file or grind a new axe to the shape and taper he preferred. With the aid of spit and hone he would whet his axe several times during each working day and grind or file it one or more times a week if nicks or burrs appeared.

Today's weekend woodchoppers use the axe more for such tasks as splitting wood and driving felling wedges than for felling, limbing, and bucking trees to the desired length. Because of this, axe selection may not be as critical. In fact, a splitting maul and wedge should be used to split wood and drive wedges, rather than an axe.

Let's assume, however, that you are like many who find working in the woods a pleasant escape from the noise and complications of modern "conveniences" (possibly including

Tools for processing wood include: **A.** double-bit axe; **B.** single-bit axe; **C.** and **D.** splitting mauls; and **E.** various-size splitting wedges.

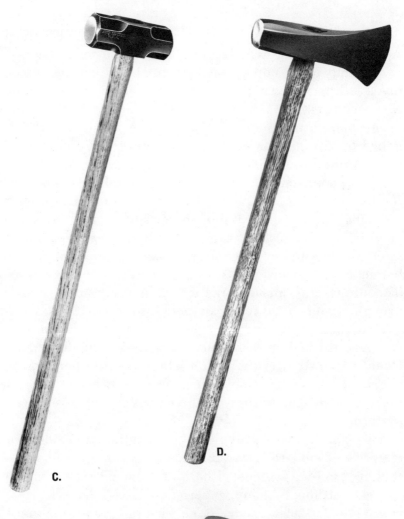

C.

D.

E.

chain saws). A single-bit axe weighing from 2½ to 3½ pounds is probably the best choice for the weekend chopper. A traditional homestead favorite, it can also safely be stuck in a stump when not in use. The single-bit can be used to drive felling wedges or for pounding stakes. Do not, however, drive metal stakes or splitting wedges with an axe, and never pound with the side of an axe. Such use can be dangerous to the user and may ruin the axe by causing it to crack around the eye.

Many people choose an axe that is too light. Actually, our forebears added weight to the early European designs, reducing fatigue by taking advantage of the axe's momentum. Also, a heavier axe, much like a sharp one, is more likely to stick to its target after a glancing blow, rather than bouncing off toward foot or leg. In addition, a heavier axe discourages the, unsafe practice of holding small trees or brush with one hand while swinging the axe with the other.

Take the time to study the various axe patterns that have survived through several decades of chain saw dominance. Usually named after the region where they first originated, commonly available single-bit axe patterns range from the narrow-bit Maine pattern to the relatively wide-bit Jersey pattern.

Also check the various handle lengths available. The majority of modern "store-bought" axes come with handles that are too long for most situations. Somewhere around 30" is best, although many experienced axe-wielders prefer shorter 26" or 28" versions, or suggest buying an axe that is "crotch high." The exacting woodchopper of old usually preferred an axe handle fashioned from fast-grown hickory. Other common and suitable woods for axe handles include white oak, red oak, sugar maple, hornbeam, and white ash.

Check the butt, or end, of the handle, remembering that the best handles will show 16 or fewer growth rings per inch, with the rings running parallel with the axe's cutting edge. The handle should also be relatively free of knots and other weakening or blister-raising defects. Avoid axes with painted handles—the paint serves no useful purpose other

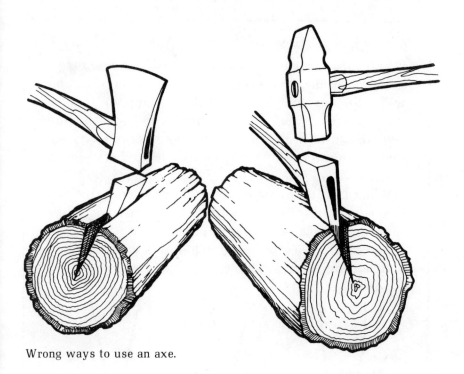

Wrong ways to use an axe.

than to disguise defects, such as the grain not running the length of the handle, as well as hiding the intrinsic beauty of the wood.

Next, check the axe to see if it has been properly matched with the handle or, in axeman's terminology, properly hung. The handle should line up with the bit when you are sighting along it. Place the bit perpendicular to a flat surface with the butt end of the handle touching the same surface. The bit of a properly hung single-bit axe will touch the surface at its mid-point or slightly behind this point toward the handle.

After buying an axe, keep in mind that the proper way to carry an axe is not over your shoulder, but at your side with the bit facing away from you, and on the downhill side when walking on steep terrain. This way you can toss it out of the way if you lose your footing.

Most axes manufactured today are too thick, with metal

How To Grind An Axe

Grind slowly on a wheel kept very wet—do not use a high-speed dry grinding wheel. Careless grinding will ruin any axe by either destroying the temper through heat caused by friction or by making the edge too thin. If a file is used for sharpening, be sure that all scratches are removed with a whetstone or hone.

When regrinding, start 2″ or 3″ back from the cutting edge and grind to about ½″ from the edge. Work for a fan shape, leaving reinforcement at the corners for strength. See cross-section pictures for the "right" and "wrong" way to shape the edge in grinding.

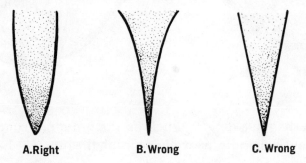

A. Right   **B. Wrong**   **C. Wrong**

Axe sharpening: **A.** Right—keep this "roll-off" convex bevel. This puts support behind the cutting edge. An axe is as thin as it should be when shipped from the factory. **B.** Wrong—this concave shape is the most common mistake in regrinding. It leaves insufficient support and will break very easily. **C.** Wrong—this long, straight bevel is better than the concave bevel but still limits the amount of support to the cutting edge.

between the bit and the eye (the eye being the point at which the handle is inserted). A few careful minutes of filing or grinding will cure this. Take care of your hands by applying a guard between the handle and file in the event of a slip, since the proper method is to file toward the bit.

An old-fashioned low-speed grindstone kept wet with

water was the favorite method of old, and is still a good approach if your shop is equipped with such an item. Never attempt to grind your axe with a high-speed electric grinder. The heat generated by this method may change the temper in an axe's metal.

Do not leave your axe out in the weather when it's not in use. At the other extreme, do not keep it in a warm, dry home where the handle will dry excessively, and possibly loosen. A dry cellar, garage, or barn is the most suitable environment for storage. If the axe does begin to loosen, an occasional tap of the butt end of the handle on a stump will secure it temporarily.

The butt end of most single-bit axe handles forms a "deer-foot," or slightly thicker, tapered section of the handle. About ¾″ of this should be cut off to create a flat surface. This enables you to secure the axe temporarily without burring the butt end of the handle. The surest cure for a loose axe, however, is to pick out the old wedge and replace it with a fresh one (never drive nails into the wedge area).

You'll probably find the factory-driven wedge to be metal. However, many people consider a wood wedge superior, particularly when it and the axe handle have been stored in a dry area. The additional moisture in the normal storage area will swell handle and wedge, resulting in an even tighter fit.

An added safeguard against the premature loosening of the axe from the handle is to drill a hole through axe and handle and install a ¼″ tension or roll pin. A small quantity of electrical tape wrapped around the handle just below the axe will reduce the amount of shock transferred along the handle to your hands. It will also lessen damage to the handle during splitting when an overextended blow brings the handle in contact with the target. Never use tape to "repair" a cracked handle.

The basics of axemanship include making sure you have a safe working area free of branches and small trees which might dangerously deflect your swing. They also include a comfortable stance to ensure firm footing. The ability to

Proper Care And Use Of An Axe

An axe is a highly specialized tool designed for chopping—take good care of it and it will give long, efficient service. Forged in one piece from a solid bar of steel, it has no seams or welds. It has been tested for defects in temper and workmanship. It is not warranted against injury by abuse or improper grinding.

Through improper grinding, the temper of the cutting edge is easily drawn or made soft, and the sidewalls weakened by grinding off the support behind the edge. Using the axe as a maul or as a wedge is a common abuse.

Good rules for using an axe include:

- Keep your axe sharp—follow proper grinding procedures.
- In cold weather, warm the axe slightly before using. Any axe with frost in it is brittle and will break with a slight blow.
- Avoid chopping into a knot or the crotch of a branch.
- When trimming branches, cut from the underside.
- Never lean your axe against a stump, tree, or wall, in or out of doors—always lay it down with the edge against the tree or wall. Protect the exposed edge of a double-bit axe.
- Stand a safe distance from a falling tree, never directly behind.
- Be extra cautious in felling a rotten tree—it is difficult to tell when or where such trees will fall.

strike the desired point with consistent accuracy and the proper amount of force is also an indication of a skilled axeman. Accuracy is the more important of the two, and results from concentration.

CHAIN SAWS

Up until the mid-sixties, the chain saw was a tool bought and used mostly by professional loggers, ranchers, and farmers. Then came the energy crunch and the rediscovery of wood as a renewable source of fuel. Result? Sales of gas chain saws skyrocketed. For example, 300,000 were sold in 1963 compared to a total sales of 2,400,000 in 1977.

Add to that figure another 650,000 electric chain saws sold in 1977 for a grand total of well over 3 million units. Major marketers of chain saws say that as sales jumped 50% from 1976 to 1977, they noted two definite trends.

A large number of buyers were first-time chain saw users, opting for smaller gas saws or electrics under $100.

Second-time buyers were choosing higher-priced, more powerful saws with a wider range of capabilities and price tags of up to $300.

The average price of chain saws has dropped significantly over the past few years. In 1970 the average selling price of a chain saw was $187. By 1977 the average price had dropped to around $160. Meanwhile, improved electric saws have reached the market, coupling valuable safety features with prices in the $50 bracket.

Any tool that's made to cut carries an inherent danger to careless or unskilled operators. Over the past decade, manufacturers have gone to great lengths to protect chain saw operators from accidents.

Probably the most significant safety innovations include anti-vibration systems and the provision of quick-stop brakes. Shock absorber mounts go a long way to reduce vibration and operation fatigue. Quick-stop brakes stop the chain when problems arise and allow you to lock the chain when not cutting, even if only to move around the tree. Other improvements contributing to safer woodcutting

Chain saws have made the job of gathering firewood faster and easier. Select the one that fits you and your needs.

include lower noise levels and designs that reduce "kick-back."

Kickback is a problem that commonly occurs when the nose of an older saw hits an immovable object and kicks back at the operator. This is a factor in at least one third of all chain saw accidents.

Some companies offer a wraparound chain brake/hand-guard which both reduces kickback and protects the operator while the saw is being used in a horizontal position, as when felling trees. Besides a full complement of safety features, there are even heated handles to prevent the operator's hands from becoming stiff in cold weather.

It's not only the more expensive models that get the benefits of safety innovations. Progressive manufacturers try to provide safety features as standard equipment on the smallest and lowest-priced saws. These are the saws generally used by the least experienced operators—homeowners who may be using a chain saw for the first time.

At least one of three factors is involved in all chain saw accidents: the environment, the operator, and the saw. The operator's skill, experience, alertness, attitude, and fatigue make the biggest difference. But manufacturers agree that selecting the right chain saw in terms of weight, balance, noise level, and vibration can go a long way to keep your woodcutting accident-free.

Buying Chain Saws

If you are buying a chain saw, make it a careful process. Most manufacturers today offer highly developed and dependable equipment, but as with any purchase, you can generally assume that price is a general indication of quality. Low-priced units are often assumed by the manufacturer to be of lighter-weight construction and not intended for the heavy-duty user. If you intend to do much cutting, buy a unit that's built for it. Check with various dealers to determine which size saw fits your needs, then compare prices on comparable saws.

The most useful gas chain saws for home wood-heating

are those with a bar length of 12" to 20". A 16" bar is a good compromise, but you might consider buying a saw that will accept a longer bar if you think you will need the extra capacity later. Anything over 25" is too large and awkward for the weekend woodcutter.

Compare saw weights only on a "loaded" basis, that is, with chain and bar in place and with oil and gas tanks filled. That's the weight it will have when you're cutting wood. Don't buy more saw than you need; too large a saw will affect your mobility and contribute to fatigue.

Also consider the power-to-weight ratio. Few chain saw manufacturers offer a horsepower rating. Keep in mind that engine displacement in cubic inches or centimeters is not the final measurement of a saw's power; some manufacturers coax more power per cubic inch from an engine.

Your best bet is to try to get the saw for a weekend test, or rent one of the same make and model before deciding to buy. Most dealers have used or demonstration saws you can test. Compare two saws with the same guide bar and chain length. Consider the balance of the saws in both felling and bucking attitudes. Good balance makes the saw feel lighter and will reduce fatigue. Also consider the advantages of a low, narrow profile, a smooth bottom, no sharp exterior corners, and no exposed linkages, oil lines, or parts to snag on brush or clothing.

Check the controls. They should be simple, positive-action, within easy reach of the control hand, and have a throttle trigger interlock. This interlock prevents the throttle from opening until the control hand is firmly in place.

All rotating parts except the chain should be enclosed. Exhaust gas and cooling air should be directed away from the operator. Check for a protective shield around the muffler to prevent burns to your skin or clothing. A chain saw should have an automatic oiler for the chain. Mechanical drive systems are considered superior. The oiler tank should be at least 40% of the capacity of the gas tank to avoid frequent refilling. Also check to see if the spark plug is located where you won't get shocks from it.

Improved safety of both gas and electrics may be one of the best reasons for chain saw owners to trade in old models for current ones.

The chain saw should start easily and have low smoke, noise, and vibration levels, which will reduce fatigue and increase saw safety. Vibration isolators should be located so that replacement is easy, and moving the saw within the vibration mounts should not cause any interference with the throttle action. Such interference could hold the throttle open at the wrong moment and cause injury to the operator.

The contour of the guide-bar nose should match the chain being used. If the guide-bar nose radius is too large, you might get a serious kickback when the nose contacts the wood. Remember that any chain that will cut wood will cut you. Some chains are designed to reduce the possibility of kickback, but are not "safety chains" in the true sense of the word.

Lightweight saws For minor cutting chores, such as pruning limbs in an orchard, the minisaw is a good choice. If you intend to use wood as a major source of heat, you'd probably be better off with a lightweight of between 9 and 12 pounds. These are more powerful, have greater utility for cutting hardwood, and come with bar lengths from 12" to 20". They usually hold a pint or so of fuel, enough to cut a half cord with one refilling.

These popular saws have good resale value, improved balance and control due to the rear-mounted handle, and a greater range of capabilities than the "mini." Many lightweight saws will accept attachments such as a brush cutter.

Medium-duty saws These saws are heavier, and of greater versatility in model choice and attachments. They are widely used in the pulpwood industry and for logging. They weigh between 12 and 16 pounds, and have engines with a capacity of up to 5 cubic inches. For the farmer, rancher, or anyone seriously cutting firewood, the medium-duty is a good choice.

Electric saws A quality electric chain saw will cost about half the price of a comparable gas model. In addition to being lighter and cheaper, they are quiet and give off no fumes. If your chain saw use is limited to trimming trees around the yard or other occasional chores, an electric can be a good choice. Newer electrics often incorporate anti-kickback features.

When you have made your selection, be sure all the tools and accessories you'll need to keep your saw maintained are included. Some of them come with the saw. Be sure to get an owner's manual and acquaint yourself with it thoroughly before filling the fuel tank. If you're handy with mechanical

Electrics cost about half as much as gas saws and can be a good choice for limited woodcutting.

things, ask the manufacturer for a shop manual so you can do your own maintenance and repairs.

Care and Use of Chain Saws

Three major things can go wrong with a chain saw.

It won't start.

It gets out of adjustment.

The chain becomes dull.

Any one of the three will put you temporarily out of business—probably when most chain saw centers are closed. With a little knowledge and less than $20 invested in a chain saw sharpener, you can make sure you can cut wood when you want to.

Chain saws are rugged tools that get a lot of work done. In so doing, however, they stir up a lot of dirt, sawdust, and grime, which all spell trouble unless you pay special attention in three areas: cleaning, adjusting, and sharpening.

Cleaning After—and sometimes during—each use you need to check the carburetor air-breather. On most saws a snap-on housing provides easy access. Remove the filter carefully so as not to dislodge dust into the carburetor and blow or brush away the dust and dirt. If the filter is very dirty you might have to soak it in solvent or gasoline. Be sure to do so in a well-ventilated area and let dry before replacing.

Check the chain and bar area near the clutch. Too much sawdust in holes and channels impedes the flow of oil to the chain—absolutely necessary for proper operation. Also check this area for foreign matter such as twigs, wood chips, and bark. This debris can work its way into the clutch housing or under the chain, and damage your saw.

Perform a visual inspection after each use. Check for loose nuts and screws. Wipe the entire saw with a soft rag. Use a small bristle brush to clean hard-to-reach areas.

Adjusting The most important thing you can do for your chain saw is to keep the correct tension on the chain. A chain that is too loose is dangerous. It could come off the bar at high speed. A chain that is too tight puts a strain on the entire system and will cause the engine to wear out much more quickly. Should the chain not get enough oil, it will become heated and will tighten up and stall the engine.

To adjust the chain to the correct tension, loosen the nut on the bar-mounting bolt just enough so that the bar will move up and down. Lift the bar upward while turning the tension-adjusting screw—clockwise to tighten, counterclockwise to loosen. The chain is correctly adjusted when it fits the bar snugly and can easily be rotated by hand.

If you are not satisfied with the idle speed of the saw, adjust accordingly. Turn adjusting screws cautiously, never more than one quarter of a turn at a time. Should you have trouble with the automatic oiler, follow instructions for adjustment in the owner's manual.

Sharpening You will learn that an investment in a precision sharpening guide will save money and time in the long run. A good guide can be purchased for less than $20.

Chain Saw Maintenance

Maintenance begins with
a general cleanup. Wipe
away sawdust, oil, and
dirt from the housing
cooling fins and the oil
and gas caps.

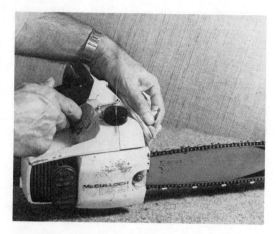

Accumulation of oil and
sawdust can restrict flow
of oil to chain. If chain
doesn't get enough oil it
can become hot, tighten
up and stall the engine, or
ruin the bar. While the
clutch housing plate is
off, remove all debris.
Wipe entire saw with a
soft rag and use a small
brush to clean hard-to-
reach areas. Check to
make sure all screws and
nuts are tight.

This chain is too loose. A
twig could throw the
chain off the bar and
cause serious injury. A
too-tight chain can ruin
the bar.

The most important part of operating a chain saw is maintaining correct chain tension. Start by loosening the bar. Unscrew the nut on the bar-mounting bolt, allowing the bar to move up and down.

To adjust the chain to proper tension, lift the bar and turn adjusting screw. Tension is correct when chain turns freely without sagging.

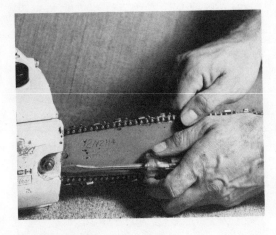

Check the starting cord. Replace it before it becomes too frayed and worn. This one is showing some wear but is still OK.

Use the recommended lubricant, not motor oil. Add oil whenever you need fuel.

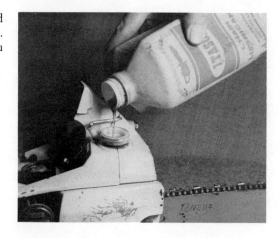

A guide makes precise sharpening easy. Secure it to the bar. A clamp holds the chain in place as you file, and can be released to move the chain.

Set the correct angle from information supplied by the manufacturer.

The next step is to adjust the file to the correct depth in the saw tooth. Be sure to file a little deeper with each sharpening.

The file is set at the correct angle and depth. The spring metal holding pawl and clamps ensure that you make a firm, straight cut with the file. Apply pressure only on the forward stroke.

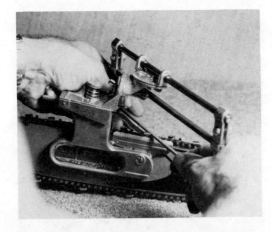

After sharpening one side, reverse the guide and sharpen the teeth on the opposite side. This is done without removing the guide from the chain and bar.

It is also possible to sharpen a chain with just a rattail file. Care should be taken to sharpen evenly or the chain will wander and bind. Many people recommend that you carry a rattail file with you in the woods and every time you take a break, spend a few minutes sharpening the teeth.

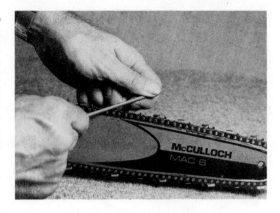

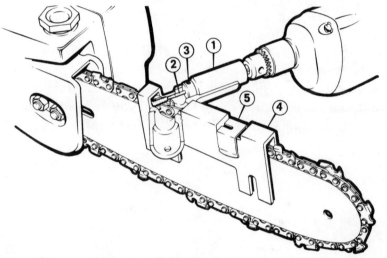

There are low-cost devices available that let you use your drill to sharpen chain saws. With this unit, grinding wheel adapter (1) is inserted into drill chuck and fitted with grinding wheel (2), using set screw (3). Grinding wheel is inserted into unit (4) which is placed over bar, where it is drawn across the saw tooth. After teeth are sharpened, saw guides are filed, using guide height gauge (5). With adapter, unit can also be used with hand file.

A guide enables you to maintain a constant, precise angle and depth as you sharpen the chain. An unevenly sharpened chain will wander in the cut and eventually bind. Some sharpening guides accept a rattail file for sharpening. Be sure you have the right size file for your saw. Apply pressure only on the forward stroke. Replace the file when dull.

To begin, clamp the guide to the bar and secure the chain in place with the spring metal pawl. Clamp the chain with the adjustable guide unit. Adjust the file to the proper angle recommended by the chain saw manufacturer. This is usually 45° or 35°. Adjust the depth gauge, remembering that you will need to file a little deeper each time you sharpen the chain.

Sharpen every other tooth. Then swing the unit around to the other side and sharpen the teeth on the opposite side.

Test your saw. It should throw out fairly large, even chips when in operation. If you get fine sawdust instead, chances are your depth gauges need to be filed slightly. If things just won't work out after resharpening, you might have it commercially sharpened to reset the angle and depth.

A few brief tips: Be sure the chain is getting oil. Use the recommended oil-gas mixture and always use fresh gas. Use chain oil made especially for chain saws. Check to ensure that you always have oil in the reservoir when the saw is in operation. Check the chain tension frequently.

3
Tips
On Cutting
Firewood

Cutting firewood can be a dangerous business, even for professionals. The chance of error is great and, as a result, every year trees claim the lives of or severely injure experienced woodsmen. Take all precautions.

CHAIN SAW SAFETY

The chain saw is a great labor-saving device for the home woodburner. It is also a potentially dangerous tool. While most chain saws have safety features, that does not mean they are safe. A common cause of chain saw accidents is kickback which can cause you to lose control of the saw. In the operation of a chain saw, engine torque is transferred to the chain. This energy is then used to cut wood. If the chain suddenly hits a solid object or takes too large a cut, and is stopped for an instant, the engine torque is transferred to the guide bar and chain saw as a rotation around the center of mass.

The direction of the reaction force depends on where the contact is made along the guide bar. If made at the upper 90° quadrant of the bar nose, the reaction will be in an upward arc toward the operator. This arcing movement of the saw blade is called kickback. Kickback is the most dangerous of the reactions that can cause loss of control.

Along the bottom rails of the bar, the reaction will be felt as a pull away from the operator. Along the top rails of the bar, the saw will tend to push toward the operator. The degree of violence with which a saw kicks back is increased by several things—dull chain, too low a chain depth gauge setting, too-loose chain tension, making chain contact at the upper quadrant of the bar nose section, and blind-cutting or boring with the bar nose at less than full throttle speed.

Anti-kickback devices on newer saws can help prevent this kickback reaction. Whether or not your saw is fitted with such a device, you should know the causes, and how to prevent kickback.

Here's how to use your chain saw to avoid kickback. First, maintain a proper stance and grip. Keep your body to the left of the guide bar. If at all possible, avoid letting the nose of the saw dip into the ground or touch obstructions. When it is necessary to bore with the saw tip, you are most vulnerable to kickback. Begin at full throttle, making first contact at the bottom quadrant of the nose section, or further back on the straight portion if there is room. When it is absolutely necessary to bore with the upper section of the nose, it is best to let a trained tree man do the job. If you are

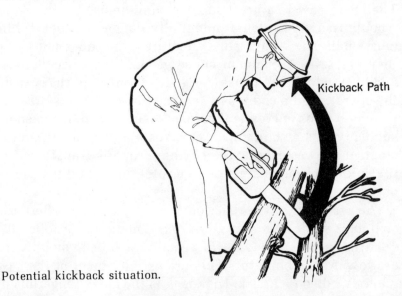

Kickback Path

Potential kickback situation.

an experienced operator, angle the saw blade to be sure that no part of your body is in the plane of chain rotation.

Limit your cutting to the range within which you can control the saw fully. Don't reach way out so you lose your balance. Don't make any cut above shoulder height, because you cannot control the saw well when it is held higher than this.

Make limbing and pruning cuts one at a time. Don't practice the tree-shearing or electric razor technique of debranching (limbing felled trees) without an anti-kickback device—you can easily hit an obstruction which will cause kickback. Whenever possible, stand on the opposite side of the tree from the branches being cut, so that the tree offers a barrier between you, the saw, and the branches.

When limbing and pruning, open the chain saw's throttle fully just before letting the chain touch the wood. It is safest to cut with the saw bumper up against the wood. If you cut further out along the bar, the chain will have a tendency to pull you and the saw toward the work. Take care to brace yourself against this slight pull. Exert light feed pressure to cut straight through the wood, but be ready to ease off on the throttle the moment the cut is completed. Safety glasses and non-slip gloves should be worn.

To cut logs with a chain saw, start the cut with the saw bumper held against log, with blade held at a slight angle. The design of the bumper on better saws gives a positive grip into the log. Open up the throttle to full speed and slowly lower the traveling chain into the log by pivoting the chain saw with its bumper kept against the log. Keep the throttle fully open throughout cutting; release the throttle as soon as the cut is completed. Protective devices fastened to the nose of some chain saw guide bars eliminate the possibility of kickback and prevent the saw from jumping back at the operator.

Remember that your hand's grip on a chain saw's handle bar is of utmost importance. Only by using the proper grip can you maintain control of the saw if it should jerk or kick

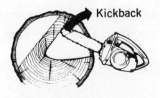

Kickback · When Incorrectly Starting to Bore

Kickback · When Nose Strikes Any Solid Object

Kickback · If Nose of Saw Hits Bottom of Saw Cut When Reinserted into Previous Cut

Situations known to cause saw to kick back toward operator.

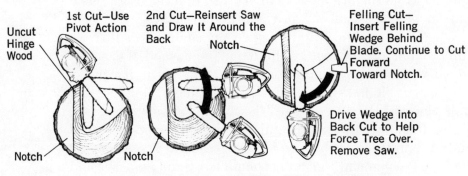

Uncut Hinge Wood

1st Cut—Use Pivot Action

2nd Cut—Reinsert Saw and Draw It Around the Back

Notch

Felling Cut—Insert Felling Wedge Behind Blade. Continue to Cut Forward Toward Notch.

Drive Wedge into Back Cut to Help Force Tree Over. Remove Saw.

Notch

Notch

Felling very large trees (up to twice bar length in diameter).

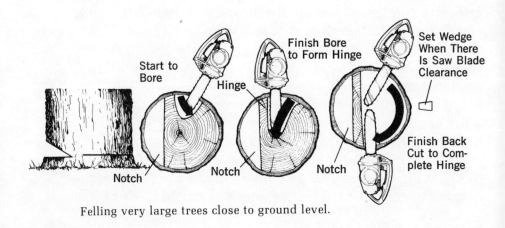

Start to Bore

Hinge

Finish Bore to Form Hinge

Set Wedge When There Is Saw Blade Clearance

Finish Back Cut to Complete Hinge

Notch

Notch

Notch

Felling very large trees close to ground level.

Your hand's grip on a chain saw's handle bar is important to maintain control of the saw if it should jerk or kick back toward you.

back toward you. Wrap your fingers around the handle bar, making sure to keep the handle bar diameter in the webbing between your index finger and thumb. Your right hand wraps naturally around the control handle.

FELLING TREES

When you feel you have the know-how, there are a few things you should check before walking up and felling your first tree.

Practice felling some small pole trees, about 6″ or smaller in diameter. While these trees don't pack the danger of the larger trees, they do demonstrate some of the dangers of felling trees. Check the wind to make sure it's blowing in the direction you want the tree to fall. Even a favorable wind can spell trouble if it's too strong; the stiller, the better.

To check which way the tree is likely to fall, go some distance from the tree and sight a pencil with the lead at the trunk and the eraser at the top. By doing so, you will be able to tell which way the tree leans. After checking three sights you should be able to determine the general direction the tree will fall. Check to make sure the downward path of the tree will not be restricted by other trees or their limbs. A hung-up tree spells danger. Get professional help to remove these trees. Don't walk under them, even if you're sure they can't fall anymore.

Trees that are on a hillside should be cut to fall down the hill. If that's not the way they are inclined to fall, leave them.

Next, check the surrounding area for any "deadheads," trees that have died but haven't fallen over. When trees hit, the ground shakes and may knock a deadhead over on you. If you check the woods thoroughly for deadheads from the start, you may find enough not to have to cut any of the potentially more dangerous living trees.

Before cutting, check your escape route. If the tree is going to fall east, plan to run northwest or southwest. Make sure you have clear sailing by removing any branches or logs in your path. The instant the tree starts to totter, drop everything and run.

When felling a tree, consider balance of tree, location of limbs, and trunk condition. Wear gloves and safety glasses, and keep your weight well balanced on both feet when cutting. Cut a notch one third of the trunk diameter and at a right angle to line of fall. Make a back cut at least 2″ higher than the notch and leave a hinge of uncut wood to guide the tree over. If there is a chance the tree might not fall correctly or may bind the saw, stop cutting before completing the back cut, and use wood or plastic wedges to open the cut and tilt the tree in the desired direction of fall.

Limbing a tree may seem like an easy operation, but it can be extremely dangerous. There are tons of pressure stored in the limbs on the underside of the tree just waiting for you to cut them loose. Start at the top of the tree, after the leaves have fallen off, and remove the small branches first. When you get to the main limbs of the tree, stand on the uphill side and cut limbs on the downhill side. Never stand on the downhill side to remove limbs.

On flat ground, one of the better ways is to cut a limb on one side, then cut another from the other side. Always cut on the opposite side of the tree. Keep your body to the left of the guide bar. You can also cut the trunk into burning lengths as you go, since the branches are holding it up.

Generally it's best to cut the limbs to 4' lengths and haul them to your splitting site, probably near your home. One of the tools used by loggers which you'll find helpful is a peavey, a pointed pole with hook used to move or roll logs. In addition, a log chain can be helpful in pulling big logs out of inaccessible places, allowing you to cut them into manageable lengths. The peavey is available at most hardware stores; if not, it can be ordered.

SAFETY CHECKLIST

The Operator

1. Wear comfortable clothing that is not loose fitting or floppy. It should not restrict your freedom of movement.

2. Good footing is extremely important—invest in a good pair of boots with steel-toe caps, sturdy leather uppers, and non-slip soles.

3. Try to use leather or special non-slip gloves to protect your hands from scratches and slivers and improve your grip on the saw.

4. Use some form of eye protection against splinters and chips. A face shield, vented goggles, or safety glasses are recommended.

5. If you are cutting standing timber a hard hat is a must. A falling limb has tremendous impact.

6. Get to know your saw. Read the owner's manual from cover to cover.

7. Work calmly and carefully. Always keep both hands firmly on the saw. Watch your footing and pay strict attention to where and what you are cutting at all times.

8. Learn to respect your saw. Use the same precautions you would use with an axe or with other power cutting tools. Don't tackle jobs beyond your capacity or experience.

9. Don't smoke near the fuel can or saw.

The Saw

1. Read the owner's manual safety section one more time.

2. Move the saw at least 20′ from where it was fueled. (Wipe any spilled fuel from the saw before you move).

3. Place the saw on a solid surface and hold firmly while you crank it. Keep the bar and chain in the clear.

4. Never carry a saw when its chain is still moving. Shut the engine off between trees (unless it has a chain-stopping system). Covering the chain with a scabbard or guard during transporation is a good idea.

5. Don't operate a saw with a loose chain. Check the chain tension frequently. Always stop the engine when adjusting chain tension. Keep the saw chain oiled, snug, and properly sharpened.

6. Use only plastic, magnesium, aluminum, or wood wedges—never iron or steel.

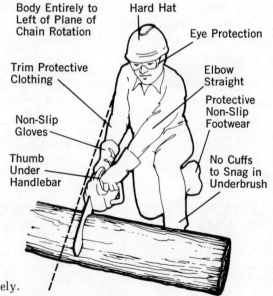

Body Entirely to Left of Plane of Chain Rotation

Hard Hat

Eye Protection

Trim Protective Clothing

Elbow Straight

Protective Non-Slip Footwear

Non-Slip Gloves

Thumb Under Handlebar

No Cuffs to Snag in Underbrush

Using a chain saw safely.

The Cutting Area

1. Keep spectators or helpers away from the operating area of the saw, and at a safe distance (2½ times tree height) when felling standing timber.

2. Make sure the saw chain is moving at full speed before you start any cut. Hold the saw bumper spike close to the material so you are not jerked forward and lose your balance.

3. Do not stand in line with the bar and chain. Learn to stand to one side of the cut while sawing.

4. Always work on the uphill side of a downed tree.

5. Look up before you start to cut any standing tree and plan both the path of tree fall and your exit path away from the tree as it starts to go over. Move quickly at a 45° angle away from the path of tree fall.

6. Always make an undercut or notch, and never cut a standing tree completely through. The "hinge" is necessary to control the direction of the fall of the tree.

7. Don't fell standing timber on windy days.

8. Be cautious of limbs under tension (bent) or compression (supporting trunk)—they can jump violently when cut, or the log can roll.

9. Limb with your feet and legs in the clear and try to keep the trunk of the tree between you and the limb being cut. Don't limb with the nose of the guide bar—kickback can result.

10. Stay alert and think about what you are doing—constantly. Don't saw in off-balance or awkward positions (overhead, at arm's length, with one hand) and don't let the bar tip get out of sight.

MAKING A SAWBUCK

If you plan to saw your own firewood, you need a sawbuck—a device to prevent the logs from rolling while you're cutting. It will require only a limited amount of bracing to saw a log with a chain saw. If you're using a crosscut or other handsaw to buck the logs, you'll exert a lot of side thrust or "push" against the sawbuck. Since the sawbuck takes a lot of rough usage, it's best to build it solid.

A sawbuck is at least two "X's" made of 2 x 4's. These are joined with cross braces. The top "V" of the "X" will hold the log; the bottom "V" of the "X" forms the legs of the buck. In constructing the "X's", three points should be kept in mind.

First, sawing will be easier if the height of the finished buck allows you to saw without bending or stooping. Take a stance as though you were cutting the wood. Drop your hands to the height you'll hold the saw. Remember that the log will be 10″ or more in diameter. Let the top "V" of the "X" be at a comfortable sawing height, so that you're not reaching up or bending down. This is also a safety factor. You want a properly balanced stance when working with a chain saw.

Second, the angle at which the 2 x 4's form the "X" will determine how large a log may fit into the top of the buck. You should spread the "V" notch of the top of the buck to the point at which it will accommodate logs of at least a 16″ diameter. Smaller logs will simply sit deeper into the "V".

A sawbuck, built like this, makes the job of handling firewood easier. Build it as strong as possible; it will take a lot of hard use.

Third, the width between the legs of the buck will establish how solidly the buck sits. The wider the stance, the more solidly the buck stands against side thrust.

If you're of average height, buy two 10′ 2 x 4's of utility grade. Cut them in half so you've got four 5′ pieces. These will form the "X's" of the sawbuck. Cross them at a point approximately two thirds of the way up the 2 x 4's. Drive a single 16d nail through them where they cross. Now spread the 2 x 4's to the proper angle to get the height and stance you desire for the finished buck. You can stand up the "X" formed by the 2 x 4's and check for height. When you determine the proper angle for the 2 x 4's to cross, put a second 16d nail in to hold the angle you want. Then spread the second "X" to match the first, and nail it too.

You can join these "X's", or legs, with 16d galvanized nails, clinching them on the backside. Or, for a buck that won't loosen and wobble, use 2½″ lag bolts.

Now cross-brace the two "X" members together, using a 5′ piece of 1 x 8. Cut it in half, so each brace (or sideplate) is 30″ long. The two "X" members will thus be 30″ apart, the length of the sawbuck. Now, using 16d nails or 2″ lag bolts, fasten the cross braces to the 2 x 4's.

Add a further cross brace to reinforce the legs of the buck. These can be 1 x 4, 2 x 4, or 1 x 6 lumber. Nail these braces across the bottom portion of the legs, at least 12″ up from the ground.

The 30″ length of the sawbuck will allow you to handle logs of 6′ or more length. When you place the log in the buck, allow at least 18″ of the log to extend past each end of the buck. You can cut off each of these overhanging ends, then make the cut at the center of the log between the "X's" of the buck. In this manner a 5′ to 6′ log can be cut into approximate 16″ lengths, a proper length for firewood.

4
How
To Prepare
Firewood

There's more to heating with wood than just felling a tree, cutting it to length, and using it as firewood. Proper splitting, drying, and storing of firewood will help you get more heat from wood, as well as make fire tending an easier job.

From 10% to 44% of the heat value of wood can be lost by burning green wood rather than letting it dry to 25% moisture content. Reason: It takes more energy to evaporate the extra moisture out of the wood. Green logs are also harder to start and keep burning.

Wood dries 10 times as fast through the ends as the sides. Cutting wood to burning length exposes more ends to the air and results in faster drying and lower moisture. After wood is cut to length, splitting logs will help them dry up to half again as fast. That's one reason it pays to fell the trees in the spring and summer when they still have leaves. Moisture is sucked out through the leaves faster than if the wood were cut and split.

Bring 4' lengths to a central location for cutting to length and splitting. While wood may dry slightly faster with the bark removed, it's not necessary to debark your logs, with the exception of diseased elm or oak which should be debarked to help stop the spread of disease to other trees.

The ideal place to store and dry firewood is in an open area with some sort of cover, with firewood supported by cement blocks or posts to prevent ground contact. A cover keeps direct rainfall and snow from soaking into the logs. Open sides ensure that the wind will blow through the logs, regardless of its direction. If the firewood is stacked on the ground, the bottom logs may rot.

There are several ways to stack firewood. One way is to stack the logs all facing the same direction with posts or trees supporting the ends. If you want a freestanding stack, lay every other layer of wood at right angle to the preceding layer. Another way is to form a square with bigger logs on the bottom and progressively smaller logs on top. Cover the top logs with branches or leaves to help shed moisture.

Square-shaped log on left has been drying for 18 months and is now ready to burn. Log on the right has been drying for two months, and the one on top was just cut. Log on right was cut using a dull chain. If you're getting ends like this, saw should be sharpened.

Either way, the more air spaces between the logs, the faster they'll dry.

For the best burning, figure on letting the wood dry one year. If you live in the South or Southwest you can have acceptable firewood in as little as three months. In the North, plan on a minimum of six months.

You can tell if wood is dry by just looking at the end of a log. Green wood shows the annual rings and the saw marks quite plainly. Wood air-dried to approximately 20% moisture will be a dull grey and have checks radiating from the center to the edge. The longer and wider the cracks, the drier the wood. Banging two pieces together can also give a clue to their relative dryness. A dull thud means too wet, while a clean ringing sound means close to correct seasoning.

SPLITTING

Unless you're planning on doing a lot of splitting, you can use a 6- or 8-pound splitting maul with a full-length handle. Because of the extra weight and the shape of the head, it splits wood much more easily than an axe. The photos show how to split wood with either this kind of maul or with wedges. If you plan to use firewood for part or all of your home heat, you may want to buy or rent a mechanical splitter.

There aren't any hard and fast rules on when it pays to buy a mechanical wood splitter. The average home, getting most of its heat from wood, will burn seven cords a year, according to the U.S. Department of Agriculture. Assuming you can get good hardwood free that otherwise is worth $50 per cord, you can pay for a $150 chain saw and a $200 mechanical wood splitter in one year. If you have to buy trees to fell, the payoff will take longer.

From a strictly economical point of view, renting is a good option. Many rental stores and chain saw dealers rent hydraulic log splitters for $25 to $35 per day. You can cut your logs to length one weekend, rent a log splitter the next weekend, and split a year's supply of firewood or more in one day.

How To Use a Wedge

With wedge, start at far side of tough wood; drive wedge in as far as it will go. On easy-to-split wood or small logs, start in center.

If a second wedge is needed, drive it in to the inside of first wedge. Log will split to free one or both of the wedges.

Log split and ready to stack. Split logs to 6" to 8" diameter. Larger logs are harder to start and keep burning.

How To Use a Splitting Maul

With a splitting maul, set log on solid base. Spread legs slightly, extend arms straight from body with log squarely in front.

On big or tough-to-split logs, aim for the far side on the first swing. Then make each successive swing closer to yourself.

On easy-to-split logs, or logs partially split, aim for the side nearest you. This helps avoid nicks and cuts on maul handle from hitting wood.

A.

B.

C.

How a hydraulic log splitter works: **A.** Log is set on pan and pull of lever starts splitting action. **B.** As hydraulic cylinder moves forward, sharp wedge splits wood. Keep hand off log when splitting, and stand back. **C.** Head of cylinders do not hit the wedge—an important safety feature. Some tough woods may not split all the way; tap on the wedge to finish the split.

Hydraulic splitters use a hydraulic cylinder to push the log into a steel wedge to split the wood. Most are designed to handle 24″ or longer logs and have enough power to split knots. Models can be powered by a tractor's hydraulic system or from their own power source. Some are available with a hydraulic jack. After setting the log on the splitter, move away and start the splitting process. Keep hands and arms away while the machine is in operation. Prices for these units range from $300 to $4,000.

Cone or screw splitters screw their way through the log until it splits. These units are available with their own

A. Cone is bolted onto rear wheel of vehicle. Rear axle is jacked up and kill switch is attached to fender. **B.** One end of log is kept on ground. With vehicle started, log is moved up to cone and splitting begins. **C.** Once log splitting is started, you can walk away if you wish to get the next log to be split. **D.** Keep hands and arms away from revolving cone. In a matter of seconds, log is split and ready for curing.

Another type of wood splitter is the jack-and-blade.

A hydraulic splitter can be mounted on the rear of a tractor.

power source, or can be mounted on the rear wheel of an automobile or garden tractor or driven by a tractor power take-off. Prices range from $200 to $400.

Jack-and-blade splitters take logs up to 12″ in diameter and 19″ to 26″ long. Logs are set on a stand and jacked into the blade. These units are designed so that every inch you move the jack causes a 2″ separation in the log. Price is about $150.

BURNING UNSEASONED WOOD

Whether you buy your firewood or get it in yourself, it is sometimes necessary to get along with wood that is less than ideally dry. Whatever the cause, most experienced fire tenders have taught themselves a few tricks for coping with the green problem. There are four main approaches, and endless combinations.

Allow more time for wet wood to cure. Time corrects unseasoned wood. Green wood will eventually become the better stack in the woodshed. Let it alone and cruise the wood lot searching for wood that is immediately fire-worthy.

In felling a dead tree there's no telling exactly what you'll get. Portions of the tree will be sound wood, but other parts may be rotted. When felling trees, be alert to dead or rotted limbs above you that may fall without warning.

Dilution may be the single most valuable way of dealing with green wood. As soon as the working woodpile of dry is half gone, it's time to begin stretching it out by mixing in occasional pieces from the fresh-cut stack. There's some penalty, but in fireplace fires a green backlog is fine for almost all times, except when you need a roaring fire or when you are laying a fire to be cared for by an inexperienced fire tender.

In stoves and heaters, green pieces in moderation are usable as make-up fuel to maintain a well-established blaze. With practice, and at a cost only of time, you'll find that adequate fires can be maintained on a diet of 30% to 40% green wood if need be.

Kindling is another answer when trying to coax a respectable blaze out of green wood. However, it takes plenty of kindling, along with time and patience. If you're short of kindling, go in the woods and look for fine shade-killed branches that protrude from the trunks of hemlock and spruce. These are particularly desirable because their elevated position has kept them from soaking on the ground in rain or under snow. The ancient rule still holds: If it snaps across your knee, it'll burn. If it bends, toss it, or put it in the sun for a few days. Collect kindling that is thumb-thick to arm-thick; smaller isn't worth your time and larger will need its own kindling wood.

Tending is a key when using green wood. Think of a fire made from unseasoned wood as if it were a misfiring car engine that won't idle but will run if you keep it moving briskly.

If you have to use green wood, split pieces one extra time, since billets that are smaller in cross section will dry out more easily in a blaze. Another trick is to increase the number of logs burning on a fire, going from three-log construction, for example, to a four- or five-log fire. If you add the extra pieces in back atop the backlog, during replenishment you can pull them forward into the blaze, adding fresh pieces in the place just vacated.

A useful variant on this trick comes in handy when you don't expect a fireplace fire to burn overnight, and when you don't look forward with enthusiasm to getting a green-wood blaze started fast in the morning chill. Load up the fire with extra wood as the evening wears on, waiting at least until the fire has cooked the extra logs to a state of burning. Then pull the fire apart, propping the logs out of the ashes against the back wall of the fireplace. Come morning they'll be messy to handle, but they'll behave as though you had seasoned wood as you hurry to get a quick blaze going.

Remember, though, that green wood has less energy available than dry wood, and that the more of it you use, the more likely you will be to have creosote buildup problems. When wood burns slowly, it produces acids that combine with moisture to form creosote. The creosote condenses and collects in the relatively cool chimney of a slow-burning fire. When ignited, creosote makes an extremely hot fire in the chimney which can endanger your home.

5
How
To Update
Older Fireplaces

The traditional fireplace has a soothing, relaxing way of warming both body and soul. Even before the fossil-fuel shortage, fireplaces added grace, charm, and warmth to houses and apartments.

All over the country, fireplaces now are being critically analyzed for their contribution to energy savings. Many, if not most, older conventional fireplaces have been found to actually waste home energy. But with energy-saving accessories now available, a fireplace can be made to complement your existing central heating system. And should storms or power failures disable a normally reliable electrical supply, your fireplace can also be used as an emergency backup for heating and cooking.

As a home heating unit, conventional unimproved fireplaces are about one-third as efficient as a woodburning stove or furnace. It's generally conceded that about 10% of the heat available in such a fireplace actually ends up heating the home. Ninety percent of the heat produced goes up the chimney. However, as this chapter points out, there are several ways to increase the efficiency of the conventional fireplace. First, a look at the basic construction of a fireplace.

FIREPLACE BASICS

The location of the fireplace within a room generally depends on the location of an existing chimney. If you are adding a fireplace, avoid locating it near doors or in the mainstream of traffic flow. Put it in the room where you spend most of your time. Take a look at some other homes that have fireplaces, noting where they're located, and ask the owners where they would locate their next fireplace and why.

The *firebox* is the area where the wood burns. The opening should be equal to or larger than the inside measurements. Fireplace openings are usually from 2' to 6' wide. Height of the opening can range from 24" for an opening 2' wide to 40" for one that is 6' wide. The higher the opening, the greater the chance of a smoky fireplace.

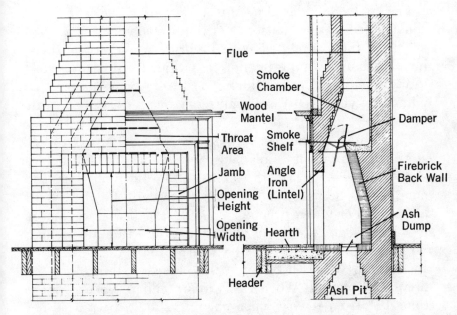

Components of a conventional fireplace. At left, elevation; at right, cross section.

In general, the wider the opening, the greater the depth. A shallow opening throws out relatively more heat than a deep one, but holds smaller pieces of wood.

The *fireplace hearth* can be made of brick, stone, terra cotta, or reinforced concrete, projecting at least 20" from the chimney breast and 24" wider than the fireplace opening (12" on each side).

The hearth can be flush with the floor so that sweepings can be brushed into the fireplace, or it can be raised. Raising the hearth to various levels and extending it in length as desired is common practice, especially in contemporary design. If there is a basement, a convenient ash dump can be built under the back of the hearth.

In buildings with wood floors, the hearth in front of the fireplace should be supported by masonry trimmer arches or other fire-resistant construction. Wood centering under the arches, used during construction of the hearth and hearth extension, should be removed when construction is completed.

The *back and sides* of a conventional fireplace are usually constructed of solid masonry or reinforced concrete at least 8" thick; they are lined with firebrick or other approved noncombustible material not less than 2" thick, or steel lining not less than ¼" thick. Such lining may be omitted when the walls are of solid masonry or reinforced concrete at least 12" thick.

The *jambs* of the fireplace are equally wide to provide stability and present a pleasing appearance. For a fireplace opening 3' wide or less, the jambs can be 12" wide if a wood mantel will be used, or 16" wide if they will be of exposed masonry. For wider fireplace openings, or if the fireplace is in a large room, the jambs should be proportionately wider. Fireplace jambs are frequently faced with ornamental brick or tile. No woodwork should be placed within 6" of the fireplace opening. Woodwork above and projecting more than 1½" from the fireplace opening should be placed not less than 12" from the top of the fireplace opening.

A *lintel* is installed across the top of a fireplace opening

4' wide or less; ½" x 3" flat steel bars, 3½" x 3½" x ¼" angle irons, or specially designed damper frames may be used. Wider openings will require heavier lintels.

If a masonry arch is used over the opening, the fireplace jambs must be heavy enough to resist the thrust of the arch.

A *throat area* of proper construction is essential for the satisfactory fireplace. The sides of the fireplace must be vertical up to the throat, which should be 6" to 8" (or more) above the bottom of the lintel.

Area of the throat must not be less than that of the flue—length must be equal to the width of the fireplace opening, and width will depend on the width of the damper frame (if a damper is installed). The sidewalls should start sloping inward to meet the flue 5" above the throat.

A *damper* consists of a cast-iron frame with a hinged lid that opens or closes to vary the throat opening. Dampers are not always installed, but they are definitely recommended, especially in cold climates. With a well-designed, properly installed damper, you can:

■ Regulate the draft.

■ Close the flue to prevent loss of heat from the room when there is no fire in the fireplace, and, in summer, to prevent insects from entering the house through the chimney.

■ Adjust the throat opening according to the type of fire to reduce loss of heat. For example, a roaring pine fire may require a full throat opening, but a slow-burning hardwood log fire may require an opening of only 1" or 2". Closing the damper to that opening will reduce loss of heat up the chimney.

Responsible manufacturers of fireplace equipment usually offer assistance in selecting a suitable damper for a given-size fireplace. It is important that the full damper opening equal the area of the flue.

The best damper controls are those designed so that the damper can be regulated from outside the fireplace. This fire control is especially important when glass doors and/or fireplace heat exchangers are used.

A *smoke shelf* prevents downdraft. It is made by setting the brickwork at the top of the throat back to the line of the flue wall for the full length of the throat. Depth of the shelf may be 6″ to 12″ or more, depending on the overall depth of the fireplace.

Ash pits are found in many fireplaces. The pit, at the back of the firebox, may be either open or have a lid. The ashes fall to a storage area in the basement or, in the case of an elevated fireplace, below the hearth. Some fireplaces have the pit opening to the outside, eliminating the chance of spilling ashes on the carpet. When using ash pits, keep in mind that a good heating fire needs a bed of coals surrounded by ashes.

TYPES OF FIREPLACES

Modified Fireplaces

These are manufactured fireplace units, made of heavy metal and designed to be set in place and concealed by brickwork or other construction. They contain all the essential fireplace parts—firebox, damper, throat, smoke shelf, and chamber. In the completed installation, only grilles show. Modified fireplaces offer two advantages.

The specially designed and proportioned firebox provides a ready-made form for the masonry, reducing the chance of faulty construction and assuring a smokeless fireplace.

When properly installed, the better-designed units heat more efficiently than brick or masonry fireplaces. They circulate heat into the cold corners of rooms and can deliver heated air through ducts to upper or adjoining rooms.

The use of a modified fireplace unit can increase the cost of a fireplace (although manufacturers claim that labor, materials, and fuel saved offset any additional cost).

Prefabricated Fireplaces

Prefab fireplaces and chimney units offer a number of advantages. A wide selection of styles, shapes, and colors are available. They offer pretested designs which are efficient in operation. They are also relatively easy to install.

They can be installed freestanding or flush against a wall in practically any part of a house.

Other advantages include light weight and lower cost than comparable masonry units. The basic part of the prefabricated fireplace is a specially insulated metal firebox shell. Since it is light in weight, it can be set directly on the floor without the heavy footing required for masonry fireplaces.

Prefabricated chimneys can be used for furnaces and heaters, as well as for prefabricated fireplaces. See the following chapter for further information.

Freestanding Fireplaces

For many, adding a masonry fireplace is too expensive, too permanent, or uses up too much space. The prefabricated freestanding fireplace is one answer.

Ben Franklin is generally credited with developing the first freestanding fireplace, and many of them today still carry his name. He developed the fireplace as an attempt to boost heating efficiency while maintaining the aesthetically pleasing sight of an open fire.

Today there are many freestanding fireplace designs, but they all incorporate three basic features: metal or cast-iron construction, portability, and open fires. Other designs allow closing off the fire with special doors which convert the unit to an airtight stove. Many units are available, in a wide variety of designs.

FIREPLACE WOOD

The key to enjoying a fireplace is a good fire, but good fires don't just happen. There is a certain expertise in laying the foundation. Knowing the basics of wood selection and fire building will enable you to build an efficient fire in no time and settle back that much sooner to enjoy it.

Selecting the type of wood for burning in your fireplace is similar to choosing a fine wine for a favorite dinner. Just as different wines are ideal for different meals, different types of wood can be used to create fires of varying heat value, aroma, and longevity. The wise fire builder will know which woods create exactly the fire he wants.

Woods that are ideal for quick, vigorous fires are called softwoods because of their resinous qualities. Pine and fir are in this category, burning rapidly and producing an extremely hot flame. Since these woods burn quickly, the fire requires frequent replenishing. Softwoods are ideal for a quick warming fire that burns out rapidly.

Extremely resinous softwoods such as hemlock and larch are not recommended for fireplace burning because they contain small pockets of moisture, even after extensive curing. As the wood begins to burn, trapped gases and moisture build up pressure and "pop," which can result in hot coals being thrown from the fire. These woods are acceptable for burning in stoves, however.

For longer-lasting fires that don't require frequent replenishing, hardwoods bring the best results. Woods in this category are ash, beech, birch, maple, and oak. All create a less vigorous fire with a shorter flame. For an extremely slow-burning fire, oak gives the most uniform flame, with steady, glowing coals.

Another group of woods is classified as aromatic. Fragrant smoke from woods such as cherry, apple, or nut generally resembles the scent of the tree's fruit. This wood is usually harder to find than hardwoods or softwoods with greater heating values, but it does produce a steady flame.

Because woods have different concentrations of resin, woody material, water, and ash, they ignite at different temperatures and have different heat values. For this reason, best results are achieved by mixing softwoods with hardwoods for an easy-to-light fire that will let you sit back for a steady show of flame. After the fire is established, adding fruitwood brings on the nostalgic aroma. (The charts in Chapter 1 can help you select wood for your fireplace.)

Kindling is a necessity for starting a fire in a conventional fireplace. Short lengths of cottonwood, aspen, fir, and pine, split to under 2″ in diameter, are recommended. Unsplit kindling should not be more than 1″ in diameter. Small twigs and branches also make ideal kindling and usually need only to be cut or broken to fireplace length before burning.

Whether you buy firewood or cut your own, a good mixture of softwoods, hardwoods, and fruitwoods backed up by a supply of kindling will give you the flexibility to build fires for any situation.

FIREPLACE TOOLS

You need only a few basic tools to help with fire tending. A poker, used to move logs apart so air spaces will remain and the fire will burn steadily, can also be used to move unburned portions of wood onto the main flame. Fire tongs are also useful for moving unburned logs onto the main flame. Other accessory tools, such as a brush and small shovel, can be used for cleanup purposes on the hearth, and in the firebox once the fire is completely out.

Bellows are helpful in replenishing a flame once new logs are added. An alternate tool to the bellows is the blowpoke, which is a hollow tube used for blowing air into the fire.

Andirons   Two andirons should be about 18″ to 24″ apart if 36″ logs are used in your fireplace. Smaller logs may require closer placement of the andirons. Use the usual "tepee" method of building a fire.

Metal grates   A grate should occupy as much of the firebox as possible, particularly the width. Grates made of several types of material are available, but those made of cast iron have best heat-retaining qualities. Logs should be laid parallel to the back wall, with crumpled paper either on top of or below the grate. Kindling should be crisscrossed between the logs for best results.

Heat-saver grates   Some heat-saver grates require little or no kindling to start a fire. If your heat saver is equipped with a glass door and a small opening below the door, no kindling is required. Place two or three softwood logs on the grate, with a ½″ stack of uncrumpled newspapers below the tubes. Turn up the edge of the top sheet of paper and light it. After the paper is burning well, close the glass doors, leaving the air intake at the base of the doors open. The rapid flow of air into the fire will ignite the wood.

HOW TO BUILD A FIRE

The basic principle to be aware of when building a fire is that easily ignitable material such as paper and kindling produces instant heat that in turn ignites larger firewood. Aside from special instructions you may receive with a heat-saver grate, the following basic fire-building method can be used either with andirons or conventional metal grates.

Start by making sure the room is well ventilated, the damper is open, and the flue unobstructed before building the fire. Poor ventilation results in slow airflow through the fire and, possibly, smoke in the room. Don't use flammable liquids to start the fire; keep other combustibles at a distance.

Make sure you have a 2″ base of ashes to serve as an insulating blanket for the bed of coals. Ashes, however, should not be allowed to cover the base of the grate, as heat buildup may eventually harm the grate and airflow through the fire is reduced.

To build a fire, place two logs on the grate parallel to the back of the fireplace. Allow a 2″ space between them for ventilation. Place crumpled newspaper and a couple of handfuls of tinder between the logs. Then place larger tinder above these pieces. Placing two more logs in a "tepee" formation above the tinder will produce a fire that starts slowly and eases through early combustion stages until logs are glowing brightly. Once the fire is burning steadily, move the logs closer together. Heat reflected between the logs helps maintain combustion temperatures and keeps the fire burning.

Maintaining a good fire is simple if these few procedures are followed.

1. Regularly adjust logs by pushing the ends into the flame. Keep the spacing between the logs small so the draft is constant. Add kindling only to revive dying coals; otherwise, add only logs.

2. Before adding new logs, rake coals toward the front of the firebox, but not past the front edge of the burning logs. Add new logs to the rear of the grate where they will reflect heat and light into the room.

3. Ashes should be left to accumulate to a depth of 2″, forming a bed for the glowing coals. They concentrate heat, and direct drafts up through the base of the fire.

4. Covering glowing logs with ashes—called "banking the fire"—can check a flaming fire for easy rekindling as much as 10 hours later. Just sift the ashes to the base of the firebox and add a small amount of kindling when you want a flaming fire again.

5. Completely open the damper when a fire is first started, then close it partway when the fire is established. The smallest damper opening can then be used when the fire is just a bed of glowing coals and you want to reduce heat loss. Never close the damper until the fire is completely out.

SAFETY TIPS

■Note that some materials should never be burned in a fireplace. Materials such as poison ivy twigs, plastics, and chemically treated poles and railroad ties may produce noxious gases. Fumes also may leave potentially dangerous deposits on flue walls and there may be sticky deposits in the ashes.

■Always keep a screen in front of the fireplace to keep sparks and hot coals in the firebox.

■Other tips: Never light a fire with flammable liquids; avoid burning wet or green wood if you can; keep a fire extinguisher handy at all times; remove combustible materials from the fireplace opening; and be careful when burning some soft, resinous woods that tend to "pop"—hot coals may be thrown from the fire.

HEAT EXCHANGERS

Heat-exchanger units for fireplaces, available in a wide assortment of designs, push heat from wood burned in the fireplace into the room.

In the conventional fireplace, outside air moves over the top of your chimney, creating an updraft, or vacuum, in the chimney. If the front of the fireplace is open, large amounts of air are forced up and out. Unfortunately, that includes most of the heat generated by the burning wood, plus some generated by your furnace. It is estimated that as much as 24,000 cubic feet of air per hour is exhausted out the chimney. (The average range is 200 to 450 cubic feet per minute.)

If your home has 1,200 square feet of floor space and the conventional 8′ ceiling height, the total cubic footage in your home is 9,600 cubic feet. This means that your house exhausts the warm air supply more than twice every hour the damper is open.

The cheapest heat exchangers to buy, and the easiest to install, are special hollow-core replacement grates. Some manufacturers say one of these units by itself can double the heat output of the fireplace. Tubular grates should be constructed of heavy-gauge steel; lightweight systems can burn out in a short time.

Such replacement grates may either depend on natural convection or use blowers. With natural convection units, cold air drawn into the bottom openings of the hollow grate is heated by the fire and forced out the top.

Installing forced-air grate systems using blowers often involves more than simply taking the old grate out and replacing it with one designed to save energy. However, companies producing units with blowers say they can boost heat production to five times greater than that of units without blowers.

You also can buy blower attachments designed to attach directly to separate hollow-core grates, as well as unitized grate systems which incorporate both mechanical airflow and glass doors into their design. Glass doors can double the heat output of a blower unit up to 100,000 Btu's per hour, enough to heat many homes.

Tubular grates for glass-door systems should use a durable metal. Stainless steel is considered excellent. The higher temperatures generated behind glass doors will cause mild steel heat exchangers to burn out rapidly. Most manufacturers recommend burning a fire in the unit only when blowers are operating. This means that the unit would be of little value during a power outage. Stainless steel tubes, however, can be used without blowers.

Claims of great savings on heating costs using various fireplace helpers may be viewed as extravagant. It is unlikely that a fireplace will generate as many Btu's as a gas furnace. No device can produce more Btu's than are contained in the wood you're burning. There are, however, devices available that will increase the efficiency of the fireplace.

The Thermograte unit pictured is an example of the natural heat convection principles and a glass door to increase efficiency. An optional blower will cause a more

Thermograte Installation
Begin by measuring the height, depth, front width, and back width (if different from the front width of the fireplace opening) to determine the correct size Thermograte unit you need.

Open both boxes and set the tubular grate and frame on its back.

Fasten the anchor straps as shown. After installing the bottom and side panels, slip the L brackets in place and finger-tighten nuts and screws.

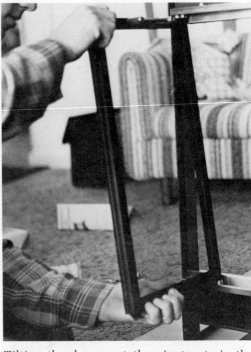

Center lower and upper door glides between side panels, pulling them as far forward as possible. The four pivot spring clips are screwed in so they're facing the outer edges.

Tilting the doors, set the pivot nuts in the pivot spring clips and the guide nuts in the door glides. The doors should fit together snugly with equal spacing on each end. Adjustments are made on the pivot spring clips.

Slide the upper and lower filigree in place. The top panel should also be installed. Make sure all panels are snug against the frame and flush with the adjoining panels before tightening all screws and nuts.

Adjust the rear leg bolts so the unit will sit level in the fireplace.

Cut the insulation to length and insert inside the top and side panels.

Slip the brass edging in place around the top and bottom. It can be installed now or after the unit is in place.

Set the assembled unit into the fireplace. Pay particular attention to fitting the bottom of the unit snug against the facing.

Mark the spot where you want to drill the holes for the lag bolts. You can then remove the unit if there isn't enough room to drill around it. Drill the holes, tap in the lead anchors, set the unit back in place, screw the lag bolts in, and you're ready for operation.

rapid airflow through the unit, increasing the amount of heat returned to the room.

Many stores have tradesmen who will install fireplace helpers for you. In most cases the units are easy to install. Typically, tools required will be a screwdriver, pliers, adjustable wrench, a hammer, electric drill, and a pencil. While installation procedures may vary somewhat from one make to another, the following will give you a general idea of how fireplace helpers are installed.

To install a unit such as this Thermograte unit, you'll need the measurement of your fireplace. Measure the height from the hearth to the top of the opening. You'll also need the depth, the width at the front of the fireplace, and the back width, if different than the front. Knowing these measurements, your dealer can recommend the best size.

Basically, the installation of a unit such as the Thermograte starts with unpacking the carton and setting the unit up according to supplied instructions. The doors, plus the bottom, left, and right side panels, are positioned and fastened. Next both upper and lower door channels are installed, followed by the unit's rear leg bolts. The legs are adjusted so the unit is level.

Before the assembled unit is set into the fire chamber, insulation is installed in the side and top panels. The insulation helps reduce air leakage around the closure and improves heating efficiency. Once the unit is into the fire chamber, the rear legs are adjusted so the top and side panels fit snugly against the facing of the fireplace. The front of the unit rests on the hearth and is anchored to it.

Note: A quarter inch of space is left between the rear wall of the fireplace and the back of the tubular grates. With less than 1/4", thermal expansion may push the unit away from the fireplace facing, allowing smoke to enter the room.

A flue handle control, which comes with the unit, can be used if reaching the old flue handle is difficult. Next the unit is anchored in place. Holes are drilled through the unit's anchor strap and into the masonry. Lead anchors are driven into the holes in the masonry, and lag bolts are used to anchor the unit down.

The first time you build a fire in your fireplace helper, some oil smoke and/or smell may be emitted from the tubes. This is because traces of oil may remain in the tubes after they have been bent at the factory. The manufacturer's instructions should tell you how to avoid this problem.

Some units with blowers use heat exchangers that mount inside your fireplace at the top. One such blower-equipped heat exchanger consists simply of a U-shaped tube about 3½" in diameter. You can also get heat-recovery units, as

Heat Exchanger Installation

This heat exchanger is a U-shaped steel tube. Fan motor is thermostatically operated and has a variable speed switch.

U-shaped clamps fit over lintel. Thumbscrews permit installation without tools.

Glued medallion sticks to fireplace or wall, and holds fan's electric cord out of firebox.

Adjustable clamps permit unit to be mounted flush to the edge of the lintel, allowing for use of screen.

well as prefab fireplaces which hook into your closed hot water system. Some generate up to 40,000 Btu's per hour.

Note: If you are planning to install a new prefab fireplace, keep in mind that most already incorporate energy-efficient designs, and also accept a variety of accessories that help you use fireplace heat to cut fuel bills. The next chapter explains how prefabs are designed and installed. Keep in mind that a relatively simple way to extract more heat from your fireplace is to replace screening with glass doors. Glass doors can earn back their cost since controlled intake draft reduces wood consumption and also offers safety from flying sparks. Glass doors are also a valuable option to consider when selecting a heat exchanger unit since they prevent heated air from re-entering the fireplace and going up the chimney.

More conventional heat exchangers on the market are similar to the one shown in the photos. The unit has five tubes for small fireplaces, and seven or nine tubes for medium and large fireplaces. Efficiency of the units is estimated by the company to be between 15,000 and 50,000 Btu's.

Air is pumped from the blower unit through a section of flex tubing to the manifold, where it is evenly distributed to each of the heavy-wall steel pipes. The fire heats the air as it moves through the tubes, and discharges into the room. The upper tubes which discharge heated air are angled out approximately 20° for wider-angle heat distribution.

A solid wood box houses the 120v blower unit, either a 100 cfm for five-tube models, or 160 cfm for larger models. The blowers have a variable speed control for adjusting the amount of heat discharge.

CONVECTOR FIREBOX

Among the assortment of devices to make your older masonry fireplace efficient is the convector box. One available model, by El Fuego, has a 12-gauge ⅛"-thick welded steel firebox with its own special damper. Your existing damper is removed. A sealing plate of sheet metal and fiber glass insulation seals off your chimney flue so the only opening is through the unit's damper. Depending on the size of your existing fireplace, from 2″ to 4″ of air space is left between the firebox insert and the masonry walls.

In operation, this type of unit offers a number of advantages over an open-hearth fireplace. With traditional masonry fireplaces, most of the heat from wood escapes up the chimney. Even when it's not being used, room air is drawn up the flue. With a high volume of air feeding the open fire, wood burns quickly and needs constant tending.

With the convector firebox installed (see illustrations), you get minimal heat escape, convected heat forced into the room, and controlled burning of the wood. Preheated room air either is diverted by the glass doors, or else travels around the firebox and is ventilated back into the room. Only a small amount of air, enough to feed the fire, enters through the air-intake vents and the space between the glass doors. This is the only air that escapes through the unit's special damper, which remains slightly open during operation.

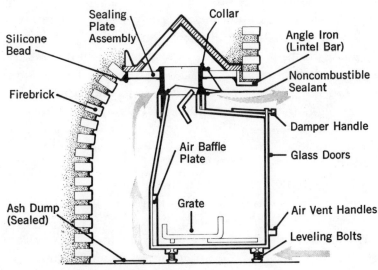

Cross section of convector firebox.

Most woodburning in the unit is done with the air-intake vents closed. This "choking" of the fire thoroughly burns firewood, leaving less ash to be carried out. (The ash dump of your existing fireplace is also sealed to prevent interference with convection currents.) Regulated airflow into and out of the firebox with external damper and air vent handles also reduces firewood consumption, so fires last longer. The design also concentrates airflow for easy starting of the fire with only a few strips of newspaper.

After the fire gets going, heat radiates to the firebrick lining of the fireplace. When the firebrick is hot, air between the unit and firebrick heats up enough to rise and to continue rising. This is the phenomenon called convection. As the air heats and rises, warmed air moves into the room through the upper grillwork; cooler air is drawn into the lower grillwork.

This type of unit has advantages. Special heat-exchanger grates, for example, can generate high Btu's either by convection or with the help of blowers. However, much of the heat generated by such units without glass doors can be drawn back into the burning fire and up the flue.

With this model, like other controlled draft units, it's easy to start fires, unless you're using green or unseasoned wood. To start a fire in this unit, first you open the damper and air vents, crumple sheets of newspaper in half, and twist and lay them between the uprights of the unit's special grate. One log, about 4" in diameter, is laid front to back, with two logs the same size laid side to side. Close the doors, and the concentrated airflow provides a bellows-like action to start the fire. No kindling is necessary, nor is it recommended.

The tempered glass doors on the firebox allow full view of the fire and also eliminate the hazards of unguarded fires, such as flying sparks, downdrafts, and rolling logs. The doors also allow less smoke and soot to reach your drapes, carpets, and furniture. And, though it's not particularly recommended, you can leave the house without putting the fire out.

Convector Firebox Installation

This convector firebox design incorporates a special air baffle plate at the rear for more efficient woodburning. Fires are built toward the rear of the unit, inside grate.

Pre-assembly check of components includes firebox, glass doors, sealing plate materials, collar, exterior frame, grate, and decorative screening.

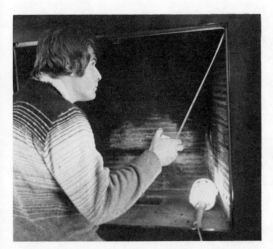

Measurements are transferred to insulation, which is used as a template for the construction of the sealing plate. Utility knife with sharp blade cuts insulation to shape.

Damper is removed and ash dump plugged. Measurements for sealing plate are taken behind angle iron or lintel of existing fireplace.

Cut insulation is checked against flue opening for accurate fit before sheet metal is attached. Making the sealing plate takes the most time.

After being measured carefully for position, the collar is placed on the insulation to mark a hole in the sealing plate which will accept the collar.

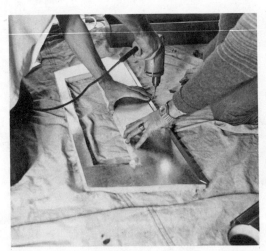

After sheet metal and insulation are cut to size, holes are drilled and U-channel galvanized sheet metal is attached around the perimeter with pop rivets.

Asbestos cement is applied to joints between sealing plate and collar, which is then inserted into sealing plate. Sealing plate is ready to install.

Sealing plate assembly is positioned and attached with sheet metal strips, which are nailed to fireplace wall and pop riveted to plate.

Joints between sealing plate and masonry walls are sealed with fire-retardant silicone sealant. Then the joints are checked for air leaks with either cigarette or candle smoke.

Flanges on firebox which accept collar (now in sealing plate) are filled with asbestos cement. Leveling leg bolts are also installed before firebox is inserted in fireplace.

With firebox inserted, collar is pulled down into flange and joints are sealed. After doors are installed, fire is started; then outside frame and decorative screening are attached.

Such a unit has a couple of small disadvantages, which are not difficult to live with. You'll miss your ash dump, which is now sealed off. You will have fewer ashes to deal with, but they must be removed more often. Chances are, however, that regular removal of ashes (a 1" bed is left on the bottom) will improve airflow and result in more efficient fires. There is another extra maintenance requirement in that the glass doors have a tendency to smoke up and must be cleaned after every few days of burning to prevent deposit buildup.

If you decide to buy a firebox insert, the first step is to measure your existing fireplace to get the right size unit. El Fuego offers three sizes, which fit practically any conventional fireplace, with openings from 30" to 48" in width and 24" or more in height. The units weigh from 120 to 145 pounds.

If your fireplace is within these dimensions, there is only one other consideration that may prevent you from using the firebox insert—excessive draft. Such units, in fact, can help solve smoky fireplace problems by considerably reducing the smoke created. However, if your draft is too great, wood in the unit may burn too fast even with the damper and air vents closed, and diminish the unit's effectiveness. Check the draft carefully if your home is on the top of a hill or if your flue is larger than 180 square inches.

The second step is to decide whether to install the unit yourself or have your dealer do it. The most difficult part is the installation of the sealer plate, which must be customized to your fireplace. Fireplaces vary so much it's virtually impossible to mass-produce this component. It can take a good two hours for an experienced installer to complete the installation. Although ordinary shop tools can be used, unless you're in the advanced handyman category or want to devote at least a full day to the job, the extra $80 to $100 it will cost you to have the unit installed will be money well spent. Here's what's involved.

1. The fireplace is cleaned and inspected for air leaks at all vertical and horizontal firebrick joints. This can be done with cigarette smoke or a candle. The ash dump is stuffed with insulation and the dump cover is sealed with asbestos cement. Then the damper flap and handle from your existing fireplace is removed. The next step, the most involved, is assembling the sealing plate.

2. Instructions with the unit give detailed guidelines on how to measure for sealing plate dimensions. The finished sealing plate consists of 1" fiber glass insulation sandwiched between galvanized sheet metal. The insulation is used as a template for the sheet metal.

3. A hole is cut in the sealing plate for the collar of the firebox. U-channel sheet metal is cut to fit the outside perimeter of the sealing plate, as well as the perimeter of the collar opening within the sealing plate. The U-channel is drilled with a ⅛" drill, pop riveted, and its joints sealed with asbestos cement.

4. Strips of galvanized sheet metal are attached with concrete nails to the sides of the fireplace to eventually hold the sealing plate in position. One strip is placed on each side of the fireplace, two at the back. The sealing plate is positioned with collar in place, and the strips are bent under it and secured with pop rivets or sheet metal screws. The perimeter of the sealing plate is then sealed with rubber silicone RTV-108 or equivalent, and checked for air leaks.

5. With the sealing plate installed, the next step is to ready the firebox for insertion. This involves adjusting strips at the top of the firebox to receive the collar (already in the sealing plate) and sealing all joints with noncombustible sealant. The legs of the firebox (actually leveling bolts which can be adjusted so the firebox will sit plumb inside your fireplace) are installed.

6. The firebox is slid into the fireplace, and the collar pulled down into the firebox neck and sealed with sealant. Then the firebox is leveled, and the grate, glass doors, and latch are installed. Before the outer frame assembly is attached, the firebox is checked by lighting a fire. Headers and legs of screening are cut to length and attached with bolts. Tabs behind the frame of the firebox hold the assembly flush against the fireplace front.

Initially the unit will give off the smell of baking paint, but only for the first two or three fires. In use, the flow of heated air at the top of the unit is not a rush of air, but a steady light flow of air 90°F or better. With four 4"-diameter logs, the unit is rated at 45,000 Btu's. But the amount of heat generated varies with the size and layout of your home, its insulation, adequacy of your original flue, the amount and quality of firewood used, and other factors.

The main and perhaps most significant advantages of the unit are that it allows you to enjoy your fireplace without wasting preheated air to feed the fire, and without wasting preheated air through an open damper while you wait for fires to go out or simply forget to close the damper.

The unit can be used without the doors with a spark screen. But if you do this, you are back to the open-hearth fireplace. The unit requires little maintenance beyond cleaning the glass doors. During summer months the unit should be cleaned and painted with high-temperature paint. This prevents moisture from mixing with the ashes and creating an acid which causes rusting.

RESTORING FIREPLACE FACINGS

Companies specializing in fireplace equipment offer a variety of components and chemicals that can help you dress the stone or brick of your fireplace, make repairs, and completely redo the facing or the hearth. One common do-it-yourself job is removing old paint from brick fireplace facings that have been painted. A sandblaster can be used, but modern solvent-type paint strippers can do the job with some elbow work.

If you plan to do this job, select a stripper strong enough to cut through successive layers of paint and full-bodied enough to cling to vertical surfaces. For an average-size fireplace, be prepared to spend a full day to complete the job.

First, assemble the materials. You'll need a water-rinsable

paint stripper, scraper, heavy steel wool, paper towels, pan, paint brush, and a box of strong detergent. Use only neoprene gloves; rubber household gloves may dissolve in the stripper. Then spread a thick layer of newspapers over any nearby flooring or finished surface. An errant dab of stripper will strip anything on which it lands. Change the papers frequently. It is even a good idea to spread a plastic drop cloth underneath the paper.

Pour a generous amount of stripper into the pan, and using the paint brush, dab it onto the brick. Get as much on as will adhere thickly to the surface. Move the brush in only one direction to get the maximum coverage. Allow the stripper to penetrate for at least 15 minutes and no more than one half hour. When the paint is completely liquified, put on neoprene gloves and scrape the surface until all the liquified paint that comes off easily is removed.

The next step is critical. Moisten a pad of heavy steel wool (a coarse wire brush is also good) with stripper and scrub the brick in a steady, vigorous, swirling motion. This action gets the stubborn paint out of the pores and completes the liquification.

Wipe off the easily removed residue with paper towels, making sure that each wipe is done with a clean towel surface. Repeat the steel wool scrub step without wiping off residue with the paper towels. After this second scrubbing the paint should be just a thin glaze or smear that is impossible to remove completely without the last step.

The remaining thin glaze of paint must be thoroughly liquified with stripper. Take a clean pad of heavy steel wool, and after soaking it in a solution of ½ cup of TSP to 1 gallon of water, scrub and rinse the remaining paint. This is the sloppiest step, but it makes the project feasible and is less sloppy than bringing a sandblaster into your living room. Wear a clean pair of old rubber gloves for the TSP step.

The complete job is rewarding because, as in other restorations, the original beauty of a natural building material is brought back to life. The old brick, which can be scarred by sandblasting or mechanical removers, is left intact.

6
Buying
And Using
Prefab Fireplaces

Many homeowners have considered adding a fireplace to their existing home but put the idea aside when they face the cost and engineering problems of traditional masonry fireplace construction. It's often the first item lost in a cutback.

The prefab fireplace is the answer in both situations. A prefab fireplace can be either freestanding (shown later in this chapter) or built in. A standard masonry fireplace can be quite expensive, especially if you're remodeling and expensive footings must be provided. Several companies now offer built-in prefab fireplace kits with price tags running less than one-third the cost.

Built-in prefabricated fireplaces are not really new. But they have been gaining rapidly in popularity during the past several years. They have earned the confidence of professional builders and are the most common type of fireplace system used in townhouses and condominiums constructed today.

Because of their light weight compared to masonry, flexibility of design, and simplicity of installation, they can be used in just about any location within any new or existing building. They can be used in multiple-level configurations, back-to-back installations, inside or outside systems. Whether installed as a single add-on to an existing home, or as part of a multi-level multi-unit installation in a large condominium, they can save the builder and the buyer considerable amounts over traditional masonry systems. Costs may be a half or a third that of masonry systems.

Because many manufacturers have entered the field of prefab fireplace construction, you, the buyer, have a great number of types and styles to choose from. Typical units are designed to be zero-clearance products. That is, they can be placed on existing combustible floors, against existing walls, or built into new construction without expensive masonry foundations.

Framing a wall around the fireplace, called "roughing in," requires only carpentry skills. At the finishing stage, brick, stone, or decorative veneers are applied to give the prefab unit the traditional fireplace appearance.

Choosing a prefab zero-clearance system involves some important considerations. First, the product should carry an

Newer prefab fireplaces offer a variety of design options for new homes or remodeling. They can be finished with real stone (left) or brick (right), imitation stone or brick, or paneling.

Fireplaces may be built with all masonry, a masonry shell that fits inside masonry, or using newer zero-clearance units. Zero-clearance units let the homeowner install a complete fireplace system himself. Basic procedure (clockwise from top left): Once unit is in place, chimney starter section is fastened. Chimney is run through ceiling to roof, with firestop fastened to top of header at ceiling. Fireplace is framed out with studs. Exterior facing is applied.

Underwriters Laboratory (UL) label. Standards and specifications for safe construction and use for this type of product have been around for some time. Most building codes require UL listing for zero-clearance fireplaces to be used. The presence of the UL listing is a good guideline to use when making a selection.

A second consideration—one that becomes important as energy costs rise—is that the unit should be able to accept glass-door closures. A fireplace without glass doors can be a heat waster. You should have the option of adding them. Some units specifically state that glass doors should not be used because they may raise firebox temperatures and, in some cases, block off special cooling vents which are designed into the system. Some manufacturers offer glass doors as an option. Check the manufacturer's literature and ask your dealer about glass doors before you make a decision.

If glass doors can be used, it may be possible to use one of the very effective fireplace heat-exchange systems in conjunction with the basic unit, to provide a heat-producing system. When selecting a unit, check the sizes of heat exchangers available and whether they will fit the prefab fireplace you're considering. To make doubly sure, check with the manufacturer to see if the units are compatible. In many cases the right combination of zero-clearance fireplace and high-quality glass-door heat exchanger can be a very good cost-effective supplementary heating system for a home.

There are also new units being made today that are classified as heat-producing fireplaces. These prefab systems, which have zero-clearance capability and usually the same flexibility of use as standard units, have built-in heat-exchange systems. Most are considerably more efficient than standard prefab fireplaces. They can make for a more rational use of the fireplace in homes where energy efficiency is desired.

A critical point to consider when comparing one heat-producing fireplace system with another is the heat output that can be achieved and the rate at which wood must be burned to produce that heat. The Fireplace Institute has recently developed standards and procedures to test and evaluate fireplace heating systems. Before you buy, check to see if this information is available.

After selection, the design and specification of a prefab system is a relatively easy task. If the location of your fireplace will allow you to install the chimney pipe straight

up, between ceiling joists and roof rafters, all you have to
know is the height measurement from the floor on which the
base of the new unit will sit to the peak of the roof of the
structure. If offsets are necessary to accommodate for ceiling joists and rafters not lining up, the amount of offset
should also be figured in. Most manufacturers provide 15°
and 30° elbows as well as a variety of chimney-section
lengths to handle almost any situation. Your dealer can help
you select the components you need and help you design the
system. Most manufacturers provide instruction guides and
templates for the do-it-yourselfer, so you can spec the whole
job if you want to.

Most persons who can hammer nails or saw wood can
install a prefab system. Most UL-listed prefabs come with
complete instructions for framing and installation. The
instructions, if followed carefully, should allow you to do a
thorough and safe job. Amazingly little time is required, and
the final effects and benefits are truly worthwhile.

When making a prefab installation, keep in mind that pipe
should never run more than 10' horizontally, and that a
system should never use more than four 30° elbows. The
chimney and any of its parts should never be more than 30°
from vertical, which means 30° bends are the maximum that
can be used.

The maximum length of angled runs should never exceed
20', and angled-run sections should be supported every 6'
Firestops must be installed in each floor through which the
flue travels. In outside or chase installations, it may be wise
to install firestop material in the area immediately above the
firebox, primarily to reduce cold-air movement around the
firebox. Sometimes insulation material such as vermiculite,
poured around the zero-clearance section of the firebox, can
help reduce cold drafts and condensation problems around
the fireplace opening.

If you can frame a partition and install paneling, you can
frame and finish a prefab fireplace.

Prefab Installation

This prefab is set between existing posts. Chimney is installed before facing is done.

With unit in place, firestop is installed. Back of unit is shown.

First section is placed on firestop. Sheet metal screws are used to join the pipe sections.

Cutout going through floor above is marked. Plywood is cut out and a metal firestop is installed.

Additional sections of pipe are aligned and fastened with screws. Here protective firestop is installed.

Elbows are attached to angle chimney through roof. Flashing, adapter, and rain cap complete installation.

SAMPLE INSTALLATION

The unit shown in the photos is a recent model introduced by Preway. It is a 42"-wide insulated unit with the back wall of the firebox built of firebrick to hold and reflect heat, a poured refractory base, and porcelainized sidewalls.

Outside air is drawn into the firebox for combustion. Cool room air is drawn into a heating chamber which is sealed off from the firebox, then heated and recirculated. Glass doors keep heated air from escaping, and radiate additional heat. The unit's circulating air system, along with the adjustable front-control damper, results in a low burn rate and more room heat per log.

A general rule of thumb when deciding what size hearth opening you need is this: Take the dimensions of the room in which you plan to locate the fireplace. Add length to width, then figure 1" of fireplace opening for each 1' of room dimension. A room of 20' x 22', for example, gives a total of 42' which would require a 42" hearth opening.

When choosing location, keep in mind that the fireplace opening should not be closer than 3" to a perpendicular wall of combustible material. If you are installing the fireplace on a wood floor, it's wise to use a 6' sheet metal strip, with half of it under the unit, half under a hearth to be constructed of noncombustible material. This prevents sparks from falling between the prefab and the hearth.

In the installation shown, the prefab was fitted in a lakeshore cabin between two posts that ran up to the rafters between a kitchen and living room. First, ¾" plywood was used to bridge across a 52" space between the posts. Feather rock was used for facing; it was attached with ceramic-tile mastic, then grouted.

Prefabricated triple-wall chimney was positioned between framing that was set on 16" centers. Additional sections were added, rotating each section until the seams aligned. A metal firestop spacer was used on the bottom of the frame openings through which the chimney passed. Although a triple-wall chimney is cool to the touch, a 1"

Finishing Off

Plywood is installed above and at sides of unit. Hearth is built to the front of opening.

Lightweight rock is applied with mastic. In this case, rock was held by countersunk finishing nails.

Hearth is built with slate laid in cement. Wire lath is used in cement to prevent cracking.

Rock dust is pressed into mastic around rocks for solid-stone appearance.

Final step is to install prefab fireplace blower unit.

clearance was allowed between the chimney and framing and flooring material.

The finished chimney was installed to be at least 3' above the roof cutout, and at least 2' above the highest point of the roof within 10' of the chimney. This height ensured a good draft.

Decorative chimney kits are available from manufacturers which can be used around the metal chimney pipe if you wish, or you can build a terminator yourself (see Chapter 9).

If you leave the metal chimney, use flashing, adapter, rain collar, and rain cap.

The prefab unit's base was outlined with 4" x 5" beams, then the area was filled with cement and filler. The hearth was finished with slate set into the cement. Trim facing can also be sheetrock, paneling, brick, stone, or ceramic tile. If your facing is a combustible material, it should be kept 5" from the sides and 7" from the top of the opening. Mantels should not be installed less than 12" from the top of the opening.

Air for combustion for this unit is drawn from the outside through a fresh-air intake duct. A saber saw was used to cut through an outside wall. The duct was then installed and sealed with caulking.

FREESTANDING PREFABS

These units are available in a wide variety of shapes, and often both the fireplace and pipe which reach to the ceiling are available in bright colors. Hoods come in conical, hexagonal, and octagonal shapes, among others. The units can be freestanding or can be installed with raised or sunken masonry hearths. Often you have a choice of hoods and trim of stainless steel, aluminum, copper, brass, baked-on enamel, or porcelain.

Freestanding prefabs radiate a complete circle of heat. Newer units, like built-in prefabs, often incorporate or accept energy-saving options such as blowers, glass doors, front draft control, and positive-seal damper.

If you have an older freestanding fireplace that doesn't offer an effective damper seal to prevent interior heat from escaping, an effective do-it-yourself solution is to make your own special sealing disc. Such a disc not only prevents heat loss in winter, but in the off-season keeps conditioned air from going up the chimney.

The photos show how a damper sealing disc is made. First measure the approximate diameter of the opening a few inches below the damper. Then use ¾" plywood or pressed wood to eliminate splitting or warping. Use all-purpose

Conical freestanding fireplaces such as this one are affordable and easy to install. They will handle any fireplace fuel and, because of their large surface areas, put out an exceptional amount of heat.

Newer freestanding units incorporate energy-saving accessories. In this model, a fan built into the back of the unit circulates air through a heating chamber and returns it to the room through side louvers.

Chimney Sealing Disc Installation

Strap iron (1" wide) forms a handle with the top part approximately two-thirds the diameter of the disc and 2" high. Drill ½" hole in the middle of handle. Screw handle securely to disc.

Place disc firmly in fireplace and measure length from handle to inside base of fireplace. Then cut a ¾" dowel 1" longer than that measurement. Taper the top ¾" of dowel to fit the ½" hole of handle.

The bottom ¼" of the dowel is angled to allow you to wedge the disc firmly into place in the fireplace. During summer the disc also helps muffle wind noises and keeps out soot dust.

sponge rubber weather stripping on the perimeter of the disc to ensure a tight seal when the disc is pushed into place inside the fireplace.

7

Buying And Using Wood Stoves

An easy way to get a serious start in using wood for home heat is to buy and install an efficient wood stove. Many homes in this country already have fireplaces, but most are only about one-third as efficient as a good wood stove.

First, some basic stove terms.

A *radiant stove*, as its name implies, radiates heat through its walls directly toward cooler surfaces in the room. The heat is absorbed by walls, floors, and ceilings, and reradiated around the room. Radiant woodburning stoves produce warmth that travels in a straight line from the heated surface. Heat is then absorbed by objects in the room, rather than heating the air directly. When used for auxiliary heating in a room, garage, or workshop, radiant heaters will supply ample heat.

Circulating stoves, sometimes called convection stoves, have primary walls surrounded by an outer jacket. Blowers, sometimes optional equipment, run off regular house current. Properly positioned, circulating heaters will provide constant, even heat throughout the home. Either of these two types may be an *airtight stove*, one whose joints are all fitted and sealed so that air enters the stove only through special vents. *Non-airtight stoves* allow some air to enter

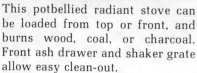

For auxiliary heating, centrally located radiant stoves can be a good choice. This unit features top loading, separate ash removal door, removable grate, and dual draft controls.

This potbellied radiant stove can be loaded from top or front, and burns wood, coal, or charcoal. Front ash drawer and shaker grate allow easy clean-out.

Radiant unit here contains 300 pounds of cast iron. Inner-sealed firebox and adjustable firedoor vent control airflow and burning rate to reduce waste and maximize burning efficiency.

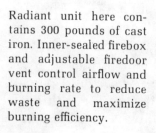

This woodburning circulating unit has airtight doors, and loads 50 pounds of wood in a 3.2-cubic-foot firebox. Heat is thermostatically controlled.

This circulating stove features automatic draft regulator, 2"-thick firebrick lining, cast-iron grates, and ash drawer for easy removal of ashes. Electric blower is optional.

Circulating heater here has ribbed bottom which allows wood to burn with adequate airflow under and over fire for constant, steady combustion; cast-iron firebox baffle plate; and automatic thermostat control. Primary combustion air enters at low point, allowing positive draft and control.

This non-airtight drum stove is a radiant stove with grate, swinging screen door, ash pan, and insulating back shield. Most drum stoves, regardless of design, are non-airtight.

Fuel efficiency is achieved in this airtight radiant stove by the front-end combustion system and the baffle, which forces the draft into an S-shaped pattern so logs slowly burn from one end to the other.

This Franklin, a non-airtight stove, may be better used as a fireplace than a primary heat source. It doubles as a cookstove with use of swing-out grille.

through joints, openings around doors, and other areas. Non-airtight stoves generally lack control over burning rates and, compared to airtight units, are not as efficient for primary home heating. Though non-airtights may be less expensive to buy, they consume wood faster, making them more costly to operate in the long run.

Some stoves, notably the Franklin, are often called fireplaces, as in the "Franklin fireplace." It is, for all practical purposes, a stove. Freestanding fireplaces, on the other hand, may be classified as either fireplaces or stoves, depending on their construction. Front-burning models, which have a door that pulls down or swings around the side to make the unit airtight, can be broadly categorized as stoves.

Many woodburning stoves can be used for light cooking. However, woodburning cookstoves are regaining popularity. Some burn coal as well as wood, and can be used for heat, hot water, and hot meals.

SELECTING A STOVE

In selecting a stove, first determine the area you want to heat, where the stove will be, and where people will be relative to the stove installation.

If you want to heat an open space, if your stove will be somewhat centrally located, and/or you expect people to be spending time in areas around or near the stove, a radiant stove design may be your best choice. Radiant stoves do not warm or dry the air as readily as circulating stoves. You'll generally feel warm and comfortable around radiant stoves.

If you want your stove positioned at one end of the house or in the basement, and you want heat to be distributed to other areas of the house, then the circulating (convection) design will be your best choice. Circulating stoves warm the air and the space they are in much more readily than radiant stoves. Because they warm the air, heat can be more evenly distributed about the home. If your home has many rooms or partitions, you will be much better off with a circulating stove. The external surface of a circulating stove is cooler,

The cooking stove below features two-hole top with solid end plate, cast-iron firebox lining, heavy-gauge rolled steel, and cast-iron braces. Bottom heat shield is of aluminized steel.

This cooking stove has a deep firebox requiring less frequent fueling, a medium-size oven with rack and temperature gauge, a porcupine back, and a divided flue construction for improved oven heating.

This circulating heater can also be used to cook foods, heat water, or make coffee. No electricity is required unless optional two-speed blower is used.

too, allowing it to be placed closer to combustible surfaces. For this reason, circulating stoves are often preferable if you have young children.

Quality and Design

After determining whether you need a circulating or a radiant stove, the next step is to consider stove quality and draft-control design. If you are serious about heating with wood, don't make the mistake of buying any of the inexpensive, usually leaky (non-airtight) stoves that have found their way onto the market. Cheaper non-airtight stoves may suffice for occasional use as garage or cabin heaters, but in general their low quality and lack of control over burning rates place them outside serious consideration for home heating.

The same advice applies to the use of the Franklin type stove and its relatives for primary home heating. Such stoves may be a fine substitute for a fireplace, but they are easily overloaded and do not have sufficient draft control to meter air correctly. They can easily be overfired, or heated beyond their capacity. In addition to safety problems, the economics of using leaky non-airtight stoves are questionable. While they may be less expensive to buy initially, the cost of the extra wood they burn (sometimes several times more than good airtights) adds up. If you cut your own wood, a good airtight stove will help save your back.

When you begin shopping for a stove, look specifically at draft control. There are two basic methods of control: manual and thermostatic (semi-automatic). The manually controlled stoves are nearly all base burners—that is, they have no grates. Most of these stoves do a surprisingly good job of holding a certain burn-rate level, which you preset. The fact that no grate is used helps to even out the burn rate, since no air gets to the fire from below.

The fire in manual draft-control stoves can be held for long burns. Coals may be present even after several days, although little heat will be given off. The best stoves with this type of draft design are made of high-quality cast iron or heavy sheet steel. Sheet steel stoves should have a firebrick (or cast-iron) lining. If there is no firebrick or cast-iron lining, you can use sand or leave ashes in the bottom of the stove to protect the base.

Thermostatically controlled stoves are usually designed to be used with grates. For best results, the grates should be of cast iron. The control is a simple bimetal strip or coil that relaxes as it is heated and contracts as it cools. In this way it can hold a preset level of heat output and thereby control the rate of burn. As the stove warms up, the bimetal control closes off the air supply; as it cools down, it allows more air in to keep it burning at the desired level.

One disadvantage of the semi-automatic control is that when the fire goes out, the draft control is usually wide open. With grated stoves this almost always means that the fire will go completely out if not fueled in time. (The best units can hold a fire at least 10 to 12 hours.) Also, draft failure can occur when thermostatic controls stick in either the closed or open position. If stuck in the closed position, it simply means no fire. If stuck open, however, the unit could be overheated.

Size

Next consider stove size. How much space is going to be heated? That question is the key to proper sizing. Many stove buyers end up with large stoves for small spaces, and then burn them at low rates, which results in creosote formation. Or they operate them normally and drive themselves out of the house with heat. If a stove is too small, the tendency is to overfire it to produce the desired heat level. The result is that the stove wears out long before it should. Stoves have a much shorter life when constantly overfired.

The best way to figure stove size is to run a heat loss calculation on the space you want to heat with wood. If you have a new home, you probably already know what the heat loss is. For most homes, this figure is approximately one third of the Btu output per hour, which is listed on your

CALCULATING YOUR HEAT NEEDS

Type of construction and amount of insulation		Lowest expected temperature of your area					
		-30°F	-20°F	-10°F	0°F	10°F	20°F
Exposed Walls	No insulation	26	24	21	18	15	13
	2" or more insulation	13	12	11	9	8	6
Ceilings	Attic above—no insulation	32	29	25	22	19	15
	Attic above—3" or more insulation	10	9	8	7	6	5
Floors	Over basement (with furnace)	0	0	0	0	0	0
	Over crawl space—no insulation	14	13	11	10	9	7
	Over crawl space—2" insulation	5	5	4	4	3	3
	On 4" concrete slab	10	9	8	7	6	5
Windows and Doors	Plain, single-glass windows, wood doors	170	150	130	120	105	85
	Storm windows and storm doors	80	70	60	55	50	40

(Source: Montgomery Ward)

This Btu heating formula can help you select the woodburning unit for your heating needs. It calculates the Btu heat loss of a single-family home, based on lowest expected temperature. Example: Omaha has an expected lowest temperature of -20°F (your weather bureau can give you the lowest expected temperature for your area). Determine heat loss for walls, ceilings, floors, and windows and doors. Multiply total square footage in each category by the correct multiplying factor from the table. Compare these figures with the Btu output for the unit you are considering.

existing furnace. Obviously heat loss depends a great deal upon climate and the weatherproofing level of your home. After you have a heat loss estimate, you can then consider stoves that will function in that output range.

Manufacturers usually suggest the rate of Btu's per hour their stoves will be capable of producing. By burning at a rate approximately one third to one half of that, you can expect good stove performance over the long run. Figuring size this way gives you reserve capacity for the coldest days, but allows you to burn at a rate high enough to provide heat for the space you want heated. Don't rely on manufacturer claims about how many rooms, square feet, or cubic feet a stove will heat. Your home is probably different enough to warrant a more scientific approach. A reliable stove dealer can help you make the correct choice.

Material

Next consider stove material. The choice between cast iron or sheet steel may be important in your decision. In truth, good radiant stoves can be made of either material. If two stoves—one of cast iron and one of sheet steel—are of equal size, weight, and design, the difference in measurable heating performance will be small.

The main difference between the two materials is that a cast-iron stove can crack under mechanical or thermal shock. It is usually cast in several pieces, requiring joint material, gaskets, and fasteners to hold it together and keep it airtight. Check these joints periodically for integrity, and regasket if signs of deterioration are evident. The main advantages of cast iron are that it does not warp at high temperatures and it has higher oxidation temperatures.

Sheet steel cannot crack from thermal or mechanical shock, but it can warp if it is overheated. The welded seams should remain airtight for a lifetime, requiring less maintenance.

If you buy a quality stove to begin with, either material should give you many years of service as long as you operate and maintain the unit with good judgment.

Overall Quality

The best sign of quality in a stove is its mass, as indicated by its weight. Radiant stoves should be heavier and sturdier than circulating stoves. Because circulators dissipate heat faster, they can be made of lighter-gauge material. But they still should weigh over 250 pounds.

Another key is in the way sections of the stove are joined together. Sheet steel stoves should have continuous welds, not just spot welds. Cast-iron stoves should have tightly fitting joints that help hold the joint compound in place.

One more point to check is loading ease. There are considerable differences in how easy stoves are to load. Most load through an opening on the front, usually near the bottom. This location helps reduce the amount of smoke that escapes into the room, but makes it harder to insert large pieces and to fill the fuel magazine completely. Top-loading stoves are easier to load and fill, but are more likely to let smoke into the room. Large doors make adding wood easier, but are more likely to smoke when the door is open. Doors smaller than the stove's fuel chamber make it harder to fill with good-size logs.

Also check the ash-removal system. Grated stoves are usually easier to clean and remove ashes from than non-grated or base-burning stoves. Grated stoves often have their own ash pan which allows you to pick up the pan, ashes and all, and carry it to a proper metal disposal container or directly outside for dumping. Non-grated stoves have no room for an ash pan, and must be cleaned with a shovel. Most kinds of wood, when burned in airtight stoves, yield about 1% to 3% of their original volume in ash. Most wood stoves will probably need to be cleaned every five to 10 days.

OPERATING PRINCIPLES

Since the days of Ben Franklin, people have been trying to devise new and more efficient ways to get heat from wood. Through all this, five basic operating designs have evolved, with as many variations as there are stove manufacturers. The operating principles described here are based on the way air moves through the stove. Individual manufacturers' deviations generally stem from efforts to make these types more efficient.

Updraft stoves allow air to enter through inlets at the bottom of the stove. Air then moves up through the grates into the burning wood and out the flue. Most potbellied stoves operate on this principle. You can recognize an updraft stove by its tall cylindrical or rectangular shape. If the stove is airtight, a secondary air inlet above the wood may help produce more complete combustion of the gases if the stove is burning at a high rate. An updraft stove that's not airtight generally will draw more air than necessary.

Diagonal stoves have air entering the bottom of the stove and then moving diagonally through the wood to the flue in the back of the stove. This pattern is typical of most box and drum stoves. A secondary air inlet above the wood may, again, help complete combustion on these stoves.

Diagonal stoves, as well as some other types, may have a "smoke chamber" which allows additional heat to radiate into the room. One model has an arched chamber to improve heating efficiency. Other designs include simple metal boxes and drums.

Some airtight diagonal-flow stoves have a preheating channel located at the front of the stove. Fresh air is heated as it enters this channel, then moves down and into the fire. Preheating the air may help these stoves provide a good, steady supply of heat. With a big charge of wood, they may burn all night long.

Cross-draft stoves have air entering the combustion area near the bottom and exiting near the bottom of the back of the stove. Gases passing through the hot flames are burned if there is enough oxygen.

Downdraft stoves, like cross-draft stoves, nearly always require a damper near the top of the smoke chamber to keep smoke from entering the room when the door is opened. There is a direct route from the top of the fuel chamber to the chimney when this damper is open. As more air is supplied to the fire the smoke tends to be sucked out of the chamber instead of blowing into the room.

The downdraft stove operates on the principle that if bringing the gases close to the burning wood is good, forcing them down through the burning wood should be even better. Recent modifications allow air to enter above the fire but below the top of the logs. The draft then forces the gases down and back toward the rear.

This draft pattern keeps the heat of the fire from rising through the logs, keeping the logs from burning until they have dropped down into a position to burn. As a result, a large pile of logs can't cool off the fire and, consequently, the wood burns longer.

Some downdraft stoves have heat-exchange chambers operated by a fan that sucks the hot air out into the room. The fan automatically shuts off when the stove is set or burning at a low rate. Nearly all of these stoves are airtight.

S-draft (front-end combustion) stoves start burning logs at the front end; they gradually burn back to the other end, much like a cigar. The primary draft enters through the front and contacts the front of the logs. Unburned gases must then pass over the flames to exit in front of the baffle (or smoke shelf). As unburned gases and oxygen come in contact with each other, a high-efficiency burn is achieved when the stove is operating at high temperatures.

This burning principle works better when logs are filled to the baffle. Some front-loading stoves of this type have more than one baffle, which gives heat a better chance to enter the room.

It's difficult to say which stove design is best. There are trade-offs between the completeness of combustion and the completeness of heat transfer, which is one reason stoves of radically different designs have similar efficiencies. Combustion is almost always more complete with more air. Air is generally detrimental to heat transfer. Exceptions are those stoves with a secondary smoke chamber. The efficiency of the stoves generally ranges from 40% to 60%.

Within that range, airtight stoves are more energy efficient, regardless of type, than non-airtight stoves. Open-end stoves have the lowest efficiency.

Many stove manufacturers have extolled the virtues of the secondary combustion features of their products. Secondary combustion (the burning of volatiles given off in the combustion of wood) is an elusive phenomenon. Production of gases occurs between 500° and 750°F for most wood fuels. These temperatures are quite common in burning cycles of stoves set up to burn for long periods. These gases will not burn, however, until their temperatures reach 1100°F or more. If these temperatures can be achieved, and sufficient air is present, then true secondary combustion can take place.

In nearly all stoves made today, some secondary combustion occurs when they burn at medium to high heat-output rates. And, in turn, few if any stoves can maintain or even achieve secondary combustion when low burn rates and extended refueling cycles are used. It doesn't matter how much secondary air is available if the gases are not hot enough to burn.

While these stoves are in a secondary burning mode, it is difficult to control their heat output levels. They will necessarily run hot and may not be the best choice for heating small spaces. Where large areas and high heat demand exist, secondary burners may be a good choice.

Select a new stove on the basis of quality of construction, and availability of parts and price, preferably in that order. Get all the information you can from your dealer and ask people who have been heating with wood about their experiences. An alternative is to find used or antique wood stoves and restore them to working order.

STOVE SAFETY

The National Fire Protection Association (NFPA) has established standards to determine how close a stove can be to a wall before it needs protection.

NFPA standards allow the hearth to extend 12″ from

RECOMMENDED MINIMUM CLEARANCES
FROM COMBUSTIBLE WALLS AND CEILINGS
(Adapted from National Fire Protection Association)

	Stoves		
Type of Protection	Radiant	Circulating*	Stovepipe
Unprotected	36″	12″	18″
¼″ asbestos millboard	36″	12″	18″
¼″ asbestos millboard spaced out 1″	18″	6″	12″
28-gauge sheet metal on ¼″ asbestos millboard	18″	6″	12″
28-gauge sheet metal spaced out 1″	12″	4″	9″
28-gauge sheet metal on ⅛″ asbestos millboard spaced out 1″	12″	4″	9″

Note: Combustible materials include wood, cloth, vinyl, paper, etc. Wood covered by plaster is also considered combustible. Only masonry walls are excluded.

Distances measured under "Stoves" are clearances from the sides and rear of a stove. Slightly different standards exist for the tops and fronts of stoves, but they almost always are met in practice (stoves are rarely placed close to ceilings and the space needed in front for loading is normally more than ample for safety).

Distances measured under "Stovepipe" are clearances from a parallel wall or ceiling.

Most stoves are classified as radiant. Circulating stoves have outer jackets all around the stove with openings, usually grilled, to allow air to circulate.

*12″ is minimum clearance for stoves tested and listed for this spacing. Otherwise note manufacturer's instruction on minimum clearance, usually 24″.

either side and from the back. Most stove dealers and installers recommend that the hearth extend 18″ from the front.

NFPA standards also call for the stove to be 18″ off the floor unless the stove legs are resting on cement or bricks, in which case the stove can be 4″ from the floor. The reason for this variance is that heat tends to rise, not settle. Also, the bottom of a stove is usually protected with ashes or sand, keeping it cooler.

Stovepipe

The stovepipe should be at least the size of the flue on the stove and made of a 24-gauge corrosion-resistant steel. One (or not more than two) sweeping 90° elbows may be used.

According to the NFPA, horizontal sections of stovepipe should be no more than 75% as long as the vertical portion of the pipe. Generally, however, the shorter and straighter the stovepipe, the safer the operation. If a horizontal stovepipe is necessary, use stovepipe with corrugated ends that fit snugly, and add three sheet metal screws or the equivalent. For horizontal stovepipe spans, use hangers in the middle of every 2″ section. Keep the stovepipe 18″ from any combustible surface, with a ¼″ elevation per running foot from the stove to the chimney. Crimped ends should be pointed down to keep creosote or moisture condensate inside the system.

Before starting your stove, have the local fire inspector come out and check your chimney installation. He sees a lot of installations and knows problems you may have overlooked. Also, while only some insurance companies will require this inspection, all should be notified of a new wood stove installation. It generally won't change your rate, but some companies won't cover a house fire unless they have been notified of the change.

SYSTEM MAINTENANCE

Your stovepipe should be dismantled and thoroughly cleaned prior to each heating season. Check for holes or spots that are wearing thin, and replace that section of pipe.

Chimneys should be inspected frequently and cleaned as necessary. You can clean a chimney by using proper-sized wire brushes or by placing sections of tire or tow chains in a burlap bag, suspending the bag with a long, stout cord, and dropping the bag down the chimney. Close off the house end of the chimney pipe, then pull the burlap bag up and down repeatedly through the pipe. (This same technique can be used on masonry chimneys.) When you're satisfied that all creosote and soot have been removed, open the bottom end and remove the debris.

The stove itself should be cleaned thoroughly after each heating season—more often if you're using the stove extensively. Remove all ashes from the firepit, and wire-brush the interior of the unit to remove soot and grime. Soot is an insulator equal to asbestos, and will prevent the heat from radiating into the house. Check all dampers and vent controls to be sure they're functioning properly. You can protect them with a greaseless spray lubricant. Check the exterior shell of the stove for cracks or loose joints.

Stove paint will protect the finish, preserve the appearance, and increase the efficiency of your stove. Use a special black paint or stove-blackening fluid with high carbon content. Carbon has good heat-emission properties, allowing a maximum of heat to be transferred. Chrome or other shiny finishes tend to reflect stove heat inward, toward the fire. Some manufacturers supply high-quality stove paint in many colors to fit in with your decor.

PROBLEMS AND WHAT TO DO ABOUT THEM

■Before starting your stove, check to make sure there is an adequate supply of air available. In older homes you'll have plenty of air available, but in houses that have been built for electric heat or have been completely winterized, there may be a shortage of air for a good fire.

In such homes, air may be obtained by installing an outside vent pipe. The pipe doesn't have to enter directly into the stove, but it should be installed as close to it as possible to prevent cold drafts. Or you can simply open a window near the stove.

■ A small explosion can occur when wood has insufficient oxygen to burn completely. The wood burns at low or smoldering levels, emitting gases. When the draft or door of the stove is opened, oxygen rushes in, and the gases ignite with a bang. This condition is called backpuffing.

Backpuffing can usually be eliminated by adding less wood at a time, and in bigger pieces. Open the drafts so that the fire burns with a blaze. It is always advisable to stand to one side of the door when you open it. Do not peer into the fire until you're sure it's blazing and no possibility of backpuffing is present.

■Smoking stoves are usually caused by improper draft.

The draft depends on proper air intake into the unit, proper use of the damper in the stovepipe, sufficient chimney height above the roof ensuring a good flow of air across the top of the pipe regardless of wind direction, and the fuel you are burning. Wet and inferior grades of wood will smoke regardless of the condition or operation of your stove. Smoke-free operation can be improved by using a wood grate which allows air to circulate under the wood. (Never use grates in base-burning stoves.)

■ Smoke pullers are available to create a gentle updraft in problem installations. Basically, they consist of a sheet metal cabinet with an electric fan which creates an updraft. Chapter 9, "Care and Maintenance of Chimneys," shows how one of these units is installed.

GETTING MORE HEAT

There are various ways to get more heat out of woodburning stoves. One way is to arrange for better heat distribution; another is to reclaim heat that ordinarily would be wasted.

Getting heat out of wood is often easier than getting it distributed throughout the house. When discussing heat distribution, it's helpful to understand a few basic physics terms.

Conduction is the transmission of thermal energy in a body from molecule to molecule. *Convection* is the transmission of thermal energy by moving currents of molecules. *Radiation* is the transmission of thermal energy by electromagnetic waves.

Wood stoves provide heat primarily through radiation, which is like heat from the sun, and convection. Convection works like this. If a fire is built in a stove, the air over the stove will expand. Less-dense air is pushed upward by the colder, more dense air along the floor. As the warm air reaches the ceiling, it spreads out to the walls and, as it cools, sinks to the floor. This is *gravity convection. Forced convection* occurs when the process is aided by mechanical means, such as a blower.

To get better distribution of the heat from either a wood

Heat Reclaimer Installation

This heat reclaimer (above left) has a thermostatically operated blower. Elbows, adapters, and extra pipe were used for the installation of woodburning stove. With chimney pipe removed (above right), adapter and reclaimer were fitted on woodburning stove. Cutting pipe for length (left) requires hand snips. Adapters connect pipe to heat reclaimer.

In this installation, pipe was used to draw cold air from floor; heated air goes into hot-air duct.

The unit attached to this wood stove has heat-collecting tubes inside to capture hot air that would otherwise be wasted. Thermostatically controlled blower forces air through the hot tubes.

stove or a fireplace, you can set the blower in your forced-air furnace (if you have one) to "manual" (or "summer") so that it runs continuously. Generally, to do this, the stove or fireplace should be located where furnace air is normally circulated. Another option is to use a more direct hookup to your forced-air duct system.

Many people have considered adding devices such as stack mounted heat reclaimers to their stoves to capture waste heat that would normally be expelled up the stove-pipe and chimney. While this may be an appropriate choice for units of low efficiency, such as Franklin fireplaces, free-standing, open-front fireplaces, or leaky non-airtight stoves, it is usually not required for use with modern airtight wood-burning stoves or furnaces.

A good, efficient airtight stove usually doesn't need a stack heat exchanger. In fact, the use of such products in airtight systems can cause operational problems, increase the frequency of required maintenance, and even lead to potential chimney fire hazards.

When airtight stoves operate at low output, long duration loading cycles, the stack temperatures are already quite low. When operating in this mode, unburned gases and water vapor are exhausted up the chimney. When temperatures drop much below 300°F, condensation of these materials takes place within the stovepipe and chimney, causing creosote buildup. The stack heat reclaimer actually adds to the rate of creosote formation and, in many cases, will impede the flow of gases and smoke up the chimney because it reduces the draft of the system.

If you do buy and install a heat reclaimer, it should be operated only during high-temperature, short loading-cycle burns, when plenty of excess heat is available in the stack. For maximum operating safety, home heating experts caution that these products must be properly matched to your heating unit and correctly wired and installed. If you buy a unit and don't hire a certified technician to install the units, double-check your plans with a home heating technician to make sure the installation meets local codes and is safe under all conditions.

8
Buying
And Using
Woodburning Furnaces

Woodburning furnaces are the ultimate in wood heat. They provide more heating capacity than any woodburning stove, and have a number of other advantages.

■Using ducts or pipes, they distribute heat more evenly to every room in your home.

■They take woodburning out of living quarters and put it in your basement.

■A woodburning furnace won't steal valuable living space as a stove will.

■You can buy woodburning furnaces that also run on conventional heating fuels.

Combination furnaces that burn wood as well as gas or oil are getting a lot of attention. As long as you feed the units wood, they burn wood. But if the wood burns down and you aren't there to stoke, they switch over to gas or oil. Some multi-fuel furnaces even start the wood fire automatically so there's no need to fuss with matches and kindling. (If you intend to burn coal, it is recommended that you do so only in a cast-iron unit, following the manufacturer's recommendations.)

Woodburning furnaces do, however, also have drawbacks. The first is their initial cost. Woodburning furnaces

Multi-fuel units like this one are versatile wood-heat appliances. They run on wood and your choice of gas or fuel oil.

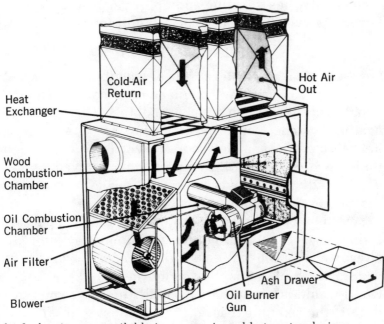

Multi-fuel units are available in warm-air and hot-water designs.

cost more than conventional gas or oil furnaces and, of course, more than wood stoves. Multi-fuel furnaces start at around $1,200 and average closer to $2,000. Furnaces that run only on wood are usually a few hundred dollars cheaper. Add the cost of installation (unless you can do the job yourself) and the money begins to add up.

Price is not the only disadvantage. With a furnace you lose much of the atmosphere and charm of wood heat. There's no stove to gather around, no cheery fire to warm your spirit. And a furnace lacks the simplicity of a good stove. When a winter ice storm knocks your power out it can also interfere with the operation of a woodburning furnace. Some furnaces cope with power outages better than other furnaces, but none can keep functioning as normally as a stove.

Before you consider buying a woodburning furnace, especially a multi-fuel unit, check to see if it is legal in your area. Many towns require furnaces to be certified by qualified agencies such as the American Gas Association, the UL, or other testing labs. In Canada it's the Canadian Standards Association. Check out your local building code. Maine, incidentally, has a testing and approval program for woodburners, so you might also check a unit for Maine approval.

BUYING A FURNACE

Once you clear up the legal side of woodburning furnaces in your area, you are ready to do some shopping. Obviously, you'll want to match your woodburner to your home's heating system. Get a warm-air furnace if you presently have forced-air heat. Get a boiler if you have hot water heat. Building a new home? Either system works well. Forced air has two advantages over hot water, however. It can accept central air conditioning and/or a humidifier.

Your next decision is not quite as simple. Should you buy a simple wood-only furnace or get a multi-fuel unit? If you already have a conventional furnace in good working order, you might think a simple woodburner would be your best bet. It would be cheaper than a multi-fuel, and you can hook it into the existing heat-distribution system. The wood

Wood-combustion chamber in unit (top) is at the right-hand side. Photo at left shows interior view of wood-combustion chamber with secondary combustion air ports at perimeter. Photo at right shows typical control hookup. Gun nozzle is set in from wood chamber but fires directly into it.

furnace and your existing furnace would act as a team, and the fossil-fuel furnace would be ready to kick in whenever the wood fire dies down.

There's only one problem. Any woodburning appliance should hook into its own double-wall, insulated chimney (Class A). It should not be vented into a flue that already

A number of companies offer complete or add-on units. This unit is an add-on pollution-free woodburning furnace that converts gas and oil warm-air furnaces into automatic multi-fuel systems. It has an independent draft regulator and automatic switchover, provides heat output of up to 200,000 Btu's per hour, holds 1000 pounds of wood, and sells for $1,195 retail.

This furnace is larger than the wood-only furnace.

serves another appliance. That means you won't be able to run the wood furnace into the chimney now serving your fossil-fuel furnace. You'll have to install a whole new chimney.

Adding a new chimney means time, money, and a certain amount of disruption in your home. Consequently, you might be better off scrapping your present furnace and opting for a whole new multi-fuel setup. The total cost might turn out to be less than you'd have to pay for the cheaper wood-only furnace plus chimney. Making your own cost comparisons will tell you which is cheaper.

If you have no need for fossil-fuel backup, then the wood-only furnace is the way to go. On the other hand, if you are building a new home or if your existing home needs a new furnace, a multi-fuel furnace is probably your best bet. Fossil-fuel backup is extremely convenient. It lets you leave your home unattended for any length of time without the danger of pipes freezing. Homeowners with only wood heat are tied to their homes through the heating season.

Multi-fuel furnaces are a good investment, even if you don't plan to heat with wood right now. You can run a multi-fuel quite efficiently on fossil fuels, but if the time ever comes when those fuels aren't available, you have that wood-heat capability standing by to get you through.

SIZING FURNACES

Buying a furnace with the right heating capacity is important. A unit that's too small will have to run overly hot to do the job, and even at that might not keep you comfortable. Oversizing, on the other hand, also lowers overall operating efficiency. All furnace makers, therefore, recommend that you determine the right size in terms of Btu's per hour before buying.

You do this by calculating the heat loss of your home. Once you know how much heat your home loses, you know how much heat the furnace has to put in. You can hire a local heating engineer to run a heat-loss calculation on your house, or you can ask the furnace maker to help you with the job. Most makers will do this for free, so take advantage of the service.

FEATURES TO CHECK

Probably the most important thing to look for in a furnace is fuel efficiency. Whether you pay for your wood or cut it yourself, you want to get every Btu possible out of that wood and into your home. There are a lot of semi-scientific claims and counterclaims about woodburning efficiency.

Basically it all burns down to this. There are two separate sides to efficiency, and both sides interrelate. The first consideration is the efficiency with which the fuel is burned—how many of the Btu's present in each log are actually released by combustion? The other consideration is the efficiency with which those Btu's are picked up and delivered to your living space.

Conditions that favor efficient combustion (fairly fast airflow and a high rate of burn), however, tend to lower the efficiency of heat transfer to your home. Conversely, conditions that favor efficient heat transfer (slow burn with minimum draft) tend to cut into combustion efficiency. So a furnace maker who stresses one side loses ground on the other. As a result, different makers may take different approaches toward optimum efficiency. But they all end up in pretty much the same area.

The most efficient wood length is in the 20" range. Longer logs (some furnaces take logs up to 5' in length) take less effort to cut, but require longer drying time, since moisture is lost most rapidly through the end grain.

Get an owner's manual for any furnace you are considering. Read through it and see how the stove operates. Does it have a separate door for ash removal? Can you remove ashes anytime, or only when the fire is almost dead? How does the furnace handle power outages? Some keep right on working on the gravity system. Others require removal of doors or plates and must be watched carefully to avoid overheating. Single loading time, the length of time the furnace will burn between refilling, depends upon the dry-ness of the wood and the energy efficiency of your house.

Also check to see if the furnace will accept a humidifier. A humidifier will let you feel comfortable at lower thermostat settings, and save you fuel all winter. Also check to see if the furnace will accept an air conditioner, and if it can be used to heat your domestic hot water supply. If it can be set up to heat water, you naturally will save money on your heating bills.

There are other points to check on multi-fuel furnaces. Is the wood fire started automatically by the oil or gas burner, or do you have to light it yourself? Do you have separate

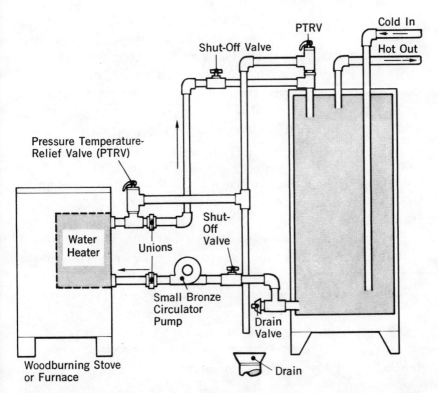

Wood furnaces can heat both domestic hot water and your home. Here's how one model gets the job done. The pressure temperature-relief valves relieve excess pressure to prevent explosions if water overheats.

combustion chambers for the wood and petroleum fuel? You should also check for a high efficiency on petroleum fuel operation. What kind of cleaning is called for? Does the unit require a lot of maintenance? Some multi-fuel furnaces are designed so they'll run perfectly well on just wood. Others are not. For example, "wood only" firing is not recommended with some units because they are designed to be used in combination with fossil fuel. Other units may be used with wood only on a temporary basis, provided care is exercised and the blower is functioning.

INSTALLING THE UNIT

If you are good with tools and have some background in electricity, there's no reason why you can't install your own wood furnace. To install a forced-air unit you'll have to be able to work with sheet metal. A hot water system will require some plumbing skills. Most furnace makers provide clear installation instructions, and dealers are helpful.

Most of the people who sell woodburning equipment believe in it. They are almost evangelical about wood heat and will go out of their way to help you get started. If you run across something in your installation that you don't know how to handle, don't hesitate to ask your dealer for help. The National Fire Protection Association also publishes two documents, NFPA 31 and NFPA 90B, which relate to the installation of solid-fuel furnaces.

The simplest installations are those that require no new chimney and no new heat-distribution system. Hooking a new furnace into an existing chimney and distribution system is not much work at all. It usually involves unpacking the furnace, a limited amount of assembly of knocked-down parts, and proper placement of the furnace close to the chimney. In some cases you will want to prepare a special concrete pad for the furnace to rest on. It's smart to read your manual and have that kind of work done before your furnace arrives.

Connecting the furnace to the chimney is critical. All makers stress the importance of locating the furnace close to its flue. Most consider 3′ the maximum allowable distance from furnace to flue. If necessary, extend the ductwork to reach the furnace, but never extend the smoke pipe beyond 3′ to reach the chimney. Make the smoke pipe run vertically as possible, avoiding 90° elbows and horizontal runs. Keep the pipe at least 18″ from all combustible surfaces.

Hooking the ductwork to the furnace may require some special fittings. Your dealer may be able to supply them, or you can have them made up at a metal shop.

Thermostat hookups and wiring for the motor or motors are detailed in the installation manuals, but vary widely from maker to maker. Sometimes you'll be using two separate thermostats, in other cases a single two-stage thermostat.

If you are planning an installation that will require a new chimney, consider using the insulated stainless steel prefab chimney. It goes together in locking sections, requires no special footings for support, and provides good performance and safety.

There is some disagreement between manufacturers regarding the method to obtain best efficiency from a wood fire. The best approach is a high burn rate, coupled with a good heat-exchange system—in other words, an efficient furnace. Low- or controlled-burn units that claim better Btu output may be doing so at the risk of high creosote buildup.

Electrical connections are just as simple. One way to handle them is to add a second thermostat (in addition to the one that already controls your furnace). This second thermostat controls only the blower in your existing furnace, not the burner section. You then set the blower for, say, 65°F, and the regular furnace for about 62°F. Whenever the temperature in your home drops to 65°F, the furnace blower will come on and force warm air from the woodburner throughout your home. If the burner can't provide enough heat and the house temperature drops to 62°F, then the main furnace will kick on and take up the slack.

A final consideration in any wood furnace installation— the wood furnace will probably require more air to breathe than your average oil or gas furnace. If your home is exceptionally well built and weather stripped, it may be too tight to let in the necessary air for combustion. In that case, the furnace will probably smoke or run poorly. The solution is to provide extra air by installing a vent to the outdoors.

FURNACE SAFETY

Burning wood is like burning any other fuel. Anytime you have a flame you have an element of risk. Probably the most important safety precaution you can take is to make sure your furnace vents to a proper chimney. You must have a Class A chimney for any woodburning appliance. This means a tile-lined masonry chimney or one of the prefab stainless steel types. If you already have an oil furnace, it will almost surely be hooked up to a Class A chimney, but that's not the case with gas furnaces.

The reason any woodburner requires a Class A chimney is creosote. Creosote is a sticky, tarlike substance that can build up inside a chimney and eventually catch fire. Only Class A chimneys can contain a chimney fire. Even then, the fire is a definite hazard, so any steps you can take to prevent creosote buildup are worthwhile.

What are those steps? First of all, burn only dry wood. Furnace makers call for wood dried to about 20% moisture content. That will require you to age your wood for a minimum of one year. Two years would be better. Allow extra time for large logs that haven't been split. Obviously a 5′ log will take longer to dry out than a 2′ log. Don't use the furnace to burn trash.

Overly cool chimney temperatures also encourage creosote production. At low temperatures the sticky stuff will condense on the chimney walls. One way to keep chimneys warm is to install them so they run inside the house, not outside. Outside chimneys lose heat to the cold outdoor air. Inside chimneys lose less heat, and what heat they do lose seeps into your home to warm it. Since they stay warmer, interior chimneys are less likely to encourage creosote, and they draw better.

If a chimney runs through an unheated attic, it will help to insulate that section of the chimney. Wrap it in foil-faced fiber glass, foil side facing the chimney. With prefab systems, this may not be permitted. Follow the manufacturer's instructions.

Another way to keep chimney temperatures higher is not to have an oversized furnace. A smaller unit will run hotter. It will also run at a continuously high level of output, so the chimney won't cool off as it would with a furnace that runs hot, then cool, then hot again. One company, for example, recommends using a boiler about 10% to 15% below the calculated heat loss for your home. During periods of extreme cold the boiler can be overfired (run full throttle) without problems. The company further recommends that the boiler be used only when outside temperatures are below 40°F. Above this temperature the furnace runs too cool to prevent creosote formation.

HELPER UNITS

Many companies that make wood or multi-fuel furnaces also manufacture smaller helper units which can be attached to forced-air systems. Units are also available to connect to hot water systems, even water heaters.

You can install units yourself if you have enough experience working with sheet metal. Installation time may be as little as a day or a day and a half. You can install a helper woodburning furnace to supplement existing heating systems for as little as $600 or as much as $1,200—or more. Price depends on brand, size, and hardware needed to mate the unit to the existing furnace.

Heating experts urge caution when buying and installing these units. Helper units can be dangerous if improperly built and installed. Check to see if the unit you are considering is listed by a qualified testing laboratory. If you don't do your own installation, contract with a qualified heating systems specialist. If you do your own installation, also check it out with a qualified heating specialist both before and after to make doubly sure the setup will be safe.

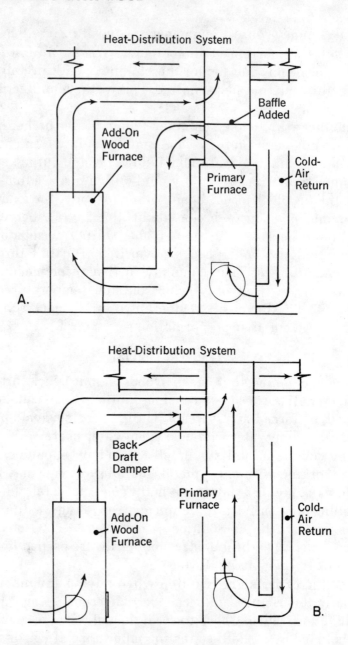

Small woodburning furnaces can be connected to your existing fossil-fuel furnace. This sample installation shows unit connected so that air heated by wood passes into heat-distribution system, not into cold-air return for main furnace. **A.** Setup without blower on woodburning furnace. **B.** Setup with blower. Installations must conform to local codes.

Heated air from the helper unit feeding into the furnace blower unit at 200°F or above can literally cook the blower's motor, and may present a fire hazard. Also keep in mind that if a helper unit's combustion chamber fails, it could result in carbon monoxide coming into your home. Therefore it is important to use only units designed for installation on the hot-air side of your existing furnace. With any helper unit, both a fail-safe thermostat control and a smoke detector are worthwhile accessories.

When buying a helper unit, pay particular attention to its construction and Btu output. Check to see how the manufacturer rates the output, and ask what the average Btu output is with a normal wood burn. Specific features to check out include:

■ Automatic damper control which varies the burning rate as the fire varies in intensity.

■ Properly sized blower system, either built into the unit or in a side-by-side mounted plenum.

■ Adequate electrical controls.

■ Good-size ash box, and heavy construction.

The liner may be either firebrick or cast iron. Brick liners are known for retaining heat and protecting steel surfaces from oxidation and corrosion. Cast-iron liners, on the other hand, can also be long wearing, and are simple to replace if needed.

Many manufacturers use caulked or asbestos-corded airtight doors; others like a small air bleed. Some design units with non-airtight doors to prevent gas buildup explosions. Unburned gases can build up inside the unit, and if the fire door is opened the onrush of oxygen may set off a blast.

The position of blower units varies by manufacturer, as do the materials you'll have to buy to complete the installation. Some units use a separate blower box; some have the blower directly attached. Sheet metal piping collars, elbows, and self-tapping chuck-head sheet metal screws which you may need are available at building material centers.

9

Care And Maintenance of Chimneys

The basics of a woodburning system include a stove or firepit, a damper system to control the draft through the chimney, the chimney itself (which in a masonry unit has flue tiles going up the center of a stone or brick surround), and the chimney terminator, which is that part of the chimney above the roof line. A metal or stone rain cap may be affixed to the top of the terminator.

A chimney serves two purposes. It carries the waste products of combustion up and out of the living area, and it provides the draft of air necessary for combustion of the fuel. The chimney may be an all-masonry unit (as in the conventional masonry fireplace), a brick/masonry chimney built to receive the stovepipe from a woodburning stove, or a prefab factory-built metal unit of two-wall insulated or three-wall insulated designs. The latter types stay cool on the outer surface, and can be used for woodburning stoves or prefab fireplaces. They may be installed almost anywhere, since little or no heat reaches nearby framing. For most UL-listed units, a 2" clearance to combustibles is necessary.

CHIMNEY BASICS

Within the house, hot air escapes through the top, while cold air is drawn into the bottom of the house. This is called the "stack effect." The house is divided into three air-pressure zones. At some point in the house, the inside air pressure will be equal to the outside air pressure, and this is called the "neutral pressure zone" (NPZ).

Above the NPZ, the air pressure is higher and pushes inside air out. Below the NPZ, the outside air pressure is higher and impedes chimney draft. A basement fireplace, below the NPZ, might smoke, while a first- or second-floor fireplace, above the NPZ, might draft properly. A chimney's capacity may be affected by the weather. In periods of high barometric pressure the chimney's draft capacity may be 20% higher than during low barometric pressures. Also, the use of venting devices such as a kitchen or bathroom vent will reduce the air pressure inside the house. If used while the fireplace is burning, they may cause the fireplace to smoke and to draft poorly.

A good grate, with plenty of space underneath for air to circulate under the fire, will allow the chimney to draft better. Glass doors also allow better control of the fire and better updraft in the fireplace, since you can control the amount of air via adjustable vents.

Masonry chimneys are usually the heaviest part of a building. They must rest on a solid foundation, such as concrete footings. Prefab chimneys are many times lighter. They need no footings, and are usually cheaper to install. They can easily be added to existing homes to provide a vent for woodburning units.

The *chimney* should extend at least 3' above flat roofs and at least 2' above a roof ridge or raised part of a roof within 10' of the chimney. A hood should be provided if a chimney cannot be built high enough above a ridge to prevent trouble from eddies caused by wind being deflected from the roof. The open ends of the hood should be parallel to the ridge.

Low-cost metal-pipe extensions are sometimes used to increase flue height, but are not as durable or as attractive as terra-cotta chimney pots or extensions. Metal extensions must be securely anchored against the wind and must have

Metal Chimney Installations

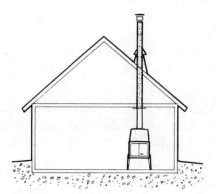

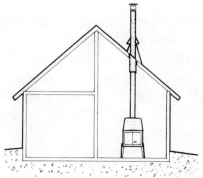

Flat ceiling with attic space. Parts needed include flush support box, roof flashing, storm collar, rain cap, and insulated pipe to reach total height.

Open-beam or cathedral ceiling. Parts needed include long support box, roof flashing, storm collar, rain cap, and insulated pipe to reach total height.

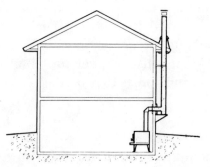

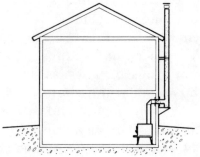

Through wall—up outside of house—through roof overhang. Parts needed include two wall or collar spacers, insulated tee, wall band or strap spacer for each 8' of wall, firestop, roof flashing, storm collar, rain cap, insulated pipe.

Through the wall—up outside of house—no roof overhang. Parts needed include two wall or collar spacers, insulated tee, tee support, wall band or strap spacer for each 8' of wall, rain cap, insulated pipe.

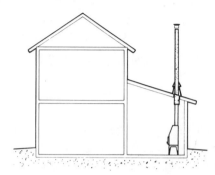

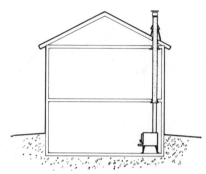

Porch or room addition with open-beam ceiling and flat roof. Parts needed include long support box, storm collar roof flashing, and insulated pipe to reach total height. *Note:* If installation is within 10′ of vertical walls, dormers, or higher roofs, increase chimney height to 2′ higher than any point 10′ away.

Multi-floor installation with flat ceilings and attic space. Parts include flush support box, firestop for each additional ceiling, roof flashing, storm collar, rain cap, and insulated pipe to reach total height.

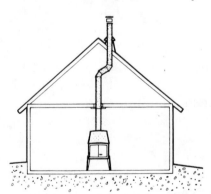

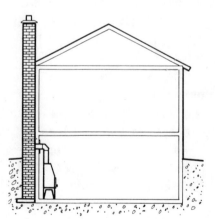

Offset installation passing ridge or obstacle in attic. Parts needed include flush support box, two insulated elbows, roof flashing, storm collar, rain cap, insulated pipe.

Through combustible wall into masonry chimney. Parts needed include two wall or collar spacers.

the same cross-sectional area as the flue. Keep in mind, however, that they can cause a great deal of creosote formation because of their cool temperatures and probably should be avoided.

The *flue* is the passage in the chimney through which air, gases, and smoke travel. Proper construction is important. Its size (area), height, shape, tightness, and smoothness determine the effectiveness of the chimney in producing adequate draft and in expelling smoke and gases.

Soundness of the flue walls may determine the safety of the building should a fire occur in the chimney. Overheated or defective flues are one of the chief causes of house fires. Manufacturers of fuel-burning equipment usually specify chimney requirements, including flue dimensions, for their equipment. Follow their recommendations.

Flue lining made of vitrified fire clay should be at least ⅝″ thick. Rectangular lining is better adapted to brick construction, but round lining is more efficient. Flues should be as nearly vertical as possible. If a change in direction is necessary, the angle should never exceed 30°. Generally the walls of chimneys with lined flues and not more than 30′ high should be at least 4″ thick if made of brick or reinforced concrete, and at least 12″ thick if made of stone.

Flue lining is recommended, especially for brick chimneys, but may be omitted if the chimney walls are made of reinforced concrete at least 6″ thick or of unreinforced concrete or brick at least 8″ thick. A minimum thickness of 8″ is recommended for the outside wall of a chimney exposed to the weather.

Openings to the flue at the roof lines are dangerous because sparks from the flue may start fires in the woodwork or roofing. Chimneys may contain more than one flue. Building codes generally require a separate flue for each fireplace, furnace, or boiler. If a chimney contains three or more lined flues, each group of two flues must be separated from the other single flue or group of two flues by brick divisions or wythes at least 3¾″ thick. Two flues grouped together without a dividing wall should have the lining joints staggered at least 7", and the joints must be completely filled with mortar.

If a chimney contains two or more unlined flues, the flues must be separated by a well-bonded wythe at least 8" thick. A soot pocket and cleanout are recommended for each flue.

No range, stove, fireplace, or other equipment should be connected to the flue for the central heating unit. Each unit should be connected to a separate flue, because if there are two or more connections to the same flue, fires may occur from sparks passing into one flue opening and out another.

Connecting pipes from furnaces, stoves, or other equipment must be correctly installed and connected to the chimney for safe operation. A smoke pipe should enter the chimney horizontally and should not extend into the flue.

The hole in the chimney wall should be lined with fire clay, or metal thimbles should be tightly built into the masonry. (Metal thimbles or flue rings are available in diameters of 6", 7", 8", 10", and 12", and in lengths of 4½", 6", 9", and 12".) To make an airtight connection where the pipe enters the wall, install a closely fitting collar and apply boiler putty, good cement mortar, or stiff clay.

A conventional smoke pipe should never be closer than 18" to woodwork or other combustible material unless properly shielded.

If a smoke pipe must pass through a wood partition, the woodwork must be protected. Either cut an opening in the partition and insert a galvanized-iron double-wall ventilating shield at least 12" larger than the pipe, or install at least 4" of brickwork or other noncombustible material around the pipe. Two-wall insulated Class A chimney sections, installed with proper 2" clearance and combustibles, will also work.

Smoke pipes should never pass through floors, closets, or concealed spaces, or enter the chimney in the attic.

SMOKE TESTS

It's a good idea to check every flue before use. Build a paper, straw, wood, or tar-paper fire at the base of the flue. When the smoke rises in a dense column, tightly block the outlet at the top of the chimney with a wet blanket. Smoke that escapes through the masonry indicates the location of leaks.

This test may show bad leaks into adjoining flues, through the walls, or between the lining and the wall. Correct defects before the chimney is used. Since such defects may be hard to correct, you should check the initial construction carefully.

Each summer when they are not in use, smoke pipes should be taken down and cleaned. When not in use, smoke-pipe holes should be closed with tight-fitting metal flue stops. Do not use papered tin. If a pipe hole is to be abandoned, fill it with bricks laid in good mortar. Such stopping can be readily removed if necessary.

CHIMNEY ACCESSORIES

Chimneys must be flashed and counterflashed to make the junction with the roof watertight. Corrosion-resistant metal, such as copper, zinc, or lead, should be used for flashing. Galvanized or tinned sheet steel requires occasional painting.

Hoods are used to keep rain out of chimneys and to prevent downdraft due to nearby buildings, trees, or other objects. Common types are the arched brick hood and the flat-stone or cast-concrete cap. If the hood covers more than one flue, it should be divided by wythes so that each flue has a separate section. The area of the hood opening for each flue must be larger than the area of the flue.

Spark arresters are recommended when burning fuels that emit sparks, such as sawdust, or when burning paper or other trash. They may be required when chimneys are on or near combustible roofs, woodland, lumber, or other combustible material. They are not recommended when burning soft coal because they may become plugged with soot.

Spark arresters do not entirely eliminate the discharge of sparks, but if properly built and installed, they greatly reduce the hazard. They should be of rust-resistant material and should have screen openings not larger than 5″ nor smaller than 5/16". (Commercially made screens that generally last for several years are available.) They should completely enclose the flue discharge area and must be securely fastened to the top of the chimney. They must be kept in position and they should be replaced when the screen openings are worn larger than normal size.

CARE AND MAINTENANCE

Most people regard masonry, brick, and the like as indestructible. They are indeed very durable. But through neglect and misuse, you can damage a chimney to the point that major repairs will be needed. And if the chimney is used while in poor condition, it may become an extreme fire hazard.

Don't burn green wood or wood that has a high moisture content. Such wood leaves a creosote deposit in the chimney flue. When creosote buildup reaches high proportions, a chimney fire can result. If possible, burn only seasoned wood.

Don't burn trash in the fireplace. Such combustibles may make a very hot fire and may clog the chimney with soot. Too hot a fire will weaken masonry joints, and a soot-clogged chimney is a hazard from both fire and fumes.

Inspect the exterior portion of your chimney yearly. Chip out and replace any loose or cracked cement in the joints. Use a mason's chisel or cold chisel, with a machinist's, mason's, or ball peen hammer (not a claw hammer) for a striking tool. Wear protective glasses to prevent chips of masonry from injuring you.

Chip out loose mortar, and brush dust and other particles from the crack. Wet the brick and adjoining mortar thoroughly before pointing the joints, to slow the absorption of water from the new cement. (Masonry cements are available in sack quantities.) Use a small pointing trowel to lay the cement into the joints. "Strike" the joints with a spoon or piece of dowel to remove the mortar down to the level of the existing joints and smooth the mortar.

Sealing Masonry

Any masonry surface should be sealed against moisture. Small cracks or checks in the surface of brick or cement will also allow water to enter. If you live in a cold climate, the water in the masonry will freeze and expand. Brick surfaces will "pop" off; mortar joints will crack or pop. Once this process begins, leaving raw brick or masonry exposed to moisture, the next soak and freeze cycle produces even more damage. If the cement cap on the chimney is cracked or pitted, mix straight portland cement into a thin paste consistency, and brush it on the cap.

When the cement joints and cap are free of cracks and all loose areas are chipped out and replaced, seal the entire masonry area with a good clear waterproofing sealer. In very severe climates, seal the chimney yearly in the fall. Masonry sealers may be brushed, rolled, or sprayed on the masonry. You can even use a garden sprayer for this purpose.

Since the top of the flashing is imbedded in the masonry joints, the flashing is difficult to replace. Clean the flashing and wipe the metal with household vinegar to neutralize the galvanizing. Then rinse with clear water, and paint with a product formulated for use over galvanized metal.

Cleaning the Flue

You can check the chimney flue to see if it's clear by looking upward, then down from the roof, through the flue. Use a flashlight or trouble light. Insertion of a mirror into a flue opening or cleanout door aids in the inspection, since it allows you to see further into the opening.

If the flue is coated with soot or creosote, have a chimney sweep clean it for you, or buy the tools to do it yourself. Several companies make tools to clean your chimney. Chemical cleaners are also available. The best tools for cleaning are specially designed brushes that fit the flue size of your systems.

Check your chimney while the fireplace is burning to see if the exterior of the chimney is warm to the touch. You should not be able to feel heat anywhere along the masonry chimney. Carefully check the area of the chimney that passes through the ceiling, into the attic, then out the roof. If it feels warm to the touch, have an expert check it. Your flue liner may be broken or damaged, and require replacement. Check for loose brick and crumbling mortar. If either is evident, your chimney may need a complete rebuild to be safe.

Wire-brush the fire pit and damper assembly. Be sure the damper operates freely and closes securely against its frame to close off the draft when the fireplace is not being used. Make sure all firebricks are tight and the masonry joints firm. If the firebricks are loose, you must use a special mortar made of fire clay to repair them. It's available from any local stone or brick dealer.

Smoke from the face brick or stone of a fireplace can be removed by washing with a trisodium phosphate solution. One tablespoon of trisodium phosphate per gallon of water is a proper ratio. If the smoke appears greasy, you can add ½ cup of household detergent to the mix.

When you're satisfied that the chimney flue is clean and the masonry in sound condition, open the damper completely. A piece of twisted newspaper or a small piece of kindling can be ignited to check the draft. The smoke should curl directly upward if the chimney is drafting properly. You may even light a newspaper to start an updraft when you've laid the wood fire. When the wood is lighted, you should have an instant updraft and avoid the smoke that some fireplaces give off when first ignited.

METAL CHIMNEYS

Used today for woodburning stoves or prefab fireplaces, these go together rapidly with a twist-lock movement.

Usually there are alignment marks on the pipes to indicate when they are locked. Some metal chimneys are secured with sheet metal screws. A simple method of installing these is to use a drill motor with a nut-runner attachment. Then buy the sheet metal screws that are self tapping so you

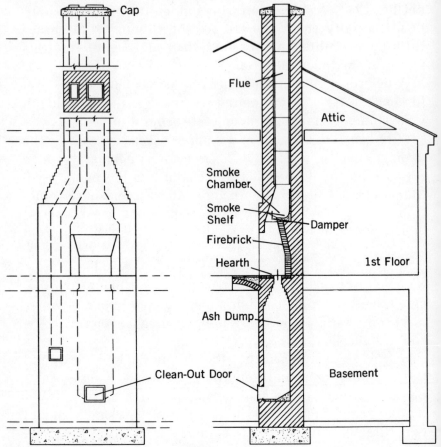

Cutaway of typical masonry chimney.

don't have to predrill holes with a bit. You can run these quickly with a power screwdriver or with a nut-runner socket in your drill.

As previously mentioned, these chimneys are designed as either two-wall or three-wall insulated systems. Either will work well. They should have the UL listing or its equivalent. Many experts feel that the two-wall insulated systems are preferable for airtight stoves because they maintain higher inside flue temperatures and are less likely to form creosote. Either system can be used, however, and the same inspection and maintenance rules apply as for any chimney system. Whatever type is used, it must be installed according to manufacturer and UL recommendations. The complete system should be installed using only the components of the system's manufacturer.

In any chimney, avoid lateral runs. The chimney should be installed as straight as possible. Any lateral or off-plumb runs restrict the draft capabilities of the chimney, and in fact are prohibited by fire codes in many cities.

Chimney Terminators

Metal chimneys can be capped with metal or artificial stone or brick terminators to give the appearance of masonry construction from the exterior. You can use chimney termination kits offered by manufacturers of prefab fireplaces. These are rectangular metal boxes which cover the chimney pipe, finished to simulate real brick. Attached to roofs with screws or screws/flashing combination, they can be cut with snips to match the pitch of the roof. Manufacturers offer these terminators at low cost.

Before laying out the framework, measure the size of the metal cover. The finished frame, including plywood, should be 1″ shorter in both width and length than the metal cover. The ½″ allowance on each side will allow the cover to extend over the brick you will apply later. Position the terminator cap so the metal chimney is at the exact center.

After determining the proper size, lay out a baseplate of

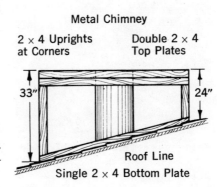

Framing detail of a terminator. Length of upright 2 x 4's is determined by roof pitch.

Metal Chimney
2 x 4 Uprights at Corners
Double 2 x 4 Top Plates
33″
24″
Roof Line
Single 2 x 4 Bottom Plate

2 x 4's on the roof. Now measure the height of the upright 2 x 4's at the top, or shorter end, of the termination base. Make this measurement from the top of the baseplate to the top of the metal chimney, less 3″. The 3″ allowance provides for the later installation of a doubled 2 x 4 top plate. Nail these two uprights into the baseplate.

Now lay a 2 x 4 over the uprights with a level on top of the 2 x 4. Level out to the longer, or lower, upright and measure the distance from the top of the plate to the bottom of the leveled 2 x 4. This will give you the length for the two longer upright 2 x 4's. Nail these two uprights at the corners of the baseplate.

You may find it easier to apply the plywood at this point than to continue with the top plate. The plywood sides will support the upright 2 x 4's, making it easier to apply the top plate. To measure the plywood that will run with the pitch of the roof, measure from the shingles to the top of the shorter upright 2 x 4's, then from the shingles to the top of the longer upright 2 x 4's. Add 3″ (to allow for the top plates) to both measurements and cut your plywood along the bias.

Example: Suppose your roof has a 3′ pitch per running

Framing is covered by ½″ plywood, which forms base. Flashing is applied at roof line.

Terminator with metal chase cover in place. Brick requires ½″ space between lip of cover and plywood.

This attractive finish on terminator conceals metal chimney pipe.

foot, the length of the termination is 3', and the chimney height at the shorter, or top, end is 2'. Your plywood side would be 3' x 2' x 33" (3" pitch p/f x 3' = 9" differential in width). Nail the sides to the upright 2 x 4's. Cut and fit both ends after nailing the sides. When applying both ends and sides to the termination, be sure to keep the upright 2 x 4 corners plumb.

Now measure and install the 2 x 4 top plates. Nail the top plate down into the corner, or upright, 2 x 4's, and nail through the plywood sides into the top plate. Next attach the metal cover, nailing through it into the top plate of the termination. Apply the flashing at the roof line. Seal both the flashing and the joint between cover and metal chimney with roof mastic.

To improve the appearance of both the metal cover and flashing, paint them before applying artificial brick. Wash the cover and flashing with vinegar, rinse thoroughly, and apply a paint formulated for galvanized application. Use a paint colored to match brick finish such as that made by Z-Brick.

Now apply the brick. Apply the mastic to the plywood,

using the coverage recommended by the manufacturer. Start the first row of brick at the top, pushing the brick underneath the metal cover. Leave ½" spaces between the rows and ends of brick to simulate masonry joints. A small brush may be supplied with the brick to smooth the mastic between joints.

At the roof line, cut the brick with a hacksaw to fit the pitch of the roof. Allow the brick to extend over the flashing by ½" to get a watertight juncture. When the mastic is dry, apply two coats of sealer to the brick.

Another method is to nail self-furring metal lath over the plywood, trowel on a coat of cement, and place feather rock into the cement. Feather rock, a lightweight volcanic rock, can be supported by nailing through the rock into the plywood, to hold until the cement sets. Drive the nails at the edges of the feather rock so the cement joints will cover the nails.

A variety of lightweight synthetic stone finishes are also available. Here again, nail self-furring metal lath over the plywood, using ¾" galvanized roofing nails. Then cover the metal lath with a layer of cement, spread the back of the stones with the cement, and place them on the plywood.

If you hold these stones for a few seconds against the cement base, they will stay in place. You can use commercially available masonry mixes, or mix your own by using a ratio of one shovel of portland cement, half a shovel of masonry cement, and three to four shovels of sand. Use the fine-screened sand called plasterer's sand.

SMOKE PROBLEMS

Fireplaces fail to draw properly for a number of reasons. A fireplace that has had much use may simply need its chimney to be cleaned. Several external problems may be the cause. A chimney top may be too low to catch the wind from all directions; obstruction may be caused by another house, a hill, or trees. A horizontal run built into the chimney itself may cause a poor draft. Or an improperly built smoke shelf or fireplace opening may preclude sufficient draft and cause the smoke to enter the house.

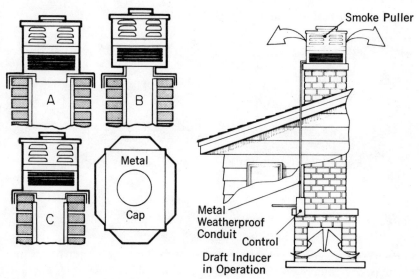

Chimney-top draft inducer fits over metal or masonry chimneys as shown in **A**, **B**, and **C**. Unit discharges in two directions. If installed on double-flue chimney, one discharge should blow across adjacent flue.

If draft problems with chimneys seem to evade your most intelligent troubleshooting, one solution may be to install commercially available smoke pullers to create an updraft. The unit shown in the photos is made by Tjernlund Products. It basically consists of a cabinet with fan. The unit is operated from a solid state speed control mounted near the fireplace. Variable speed control allows the fan speed to be adjusted to meet changing wind/fuel/temperature conditions. This unit mounts directly on an 8"-, 10"-, or 12"-diameter round metal chimney. Couplings are available to allow installation on common pipe. A sheet metal bracket may be fabricated to fit the unit on a masonry fireplace, as shown in the photos. In the case of the masonry application, apply a bead of mastic around the chimney. Then bore holes into the cement cap, using a carbide masonry bit. Insert lead anchors into the holes, and place screws into the lead anchors to hold the sheet metal bracket in place. Attach to a metal chimney using sheet metal screws.

A steel electric conduit must be run up the chimney to the entry port where the electric connection is made. To gain

Smoke Puller Installation

Sheet metal cover is fabricated to fit masonry chimney. Prefab collar from hardware store is attached to metal cover with sheet metal screws.

Roof mastic is applied around chimney flue. Note that flue has been chiseled flush to cement. Lead anchor will hold screws to fasten cover.

After screws are driven into chimney, holes of ¼″ diameter are drilled through metal and cement using carbide masonry bit.

Smoke puller installed. Wiring is installed in metal conduit attached to the exterior of the chimney (never inside chimney where it would be exposed to heat).

access to the electric wiring, you must remove the top of the unit by loosening four screws. Run #12 Romex wire up the conduit, and connect the wires to the motor. The steel conduit pipe to the outside of the house should cover all exposed wiring. Mount the control switch for the fan near the stove or fireplace. The control switch is mounted similarly to an electric outlet.

Make a continuous run of ground, or white, electrical wire from fan motor to the electricity. (The black, or "hot," wire is run from the fan unit to the electric supply, but "interrupted" by installation of a switch.) Be sure the installation conforms to your own state and local electrical codes.

The unit installs in an afternoon, and often can end a smoking fireplace problem when its fan is set at its lowest speed. Retailing for around $200, this unit offers an optional light which indicates when the motor is running—a valuable reminder to switch the unit off and close the damper when no fire is burning. Another option is the variable speed switch.

You can determine the size unit you need by figuring the face area of a fireplace. Do this by multiplying the height times the width of the opening. If the fireplace has two openings, add the two. For a woodburning stove, follow the directions of the manufacturer.

10
Questions
And Answers
On Wood Heating

Getting starting with using wood for home heating often generates basic questions which are critical to both efficiency and safety. Below are common questions asked by first-time woodburners, along with answers. If you have further questions that are not answered elsewhere in this book, don't hesitate to contact your local wood equipment dealer, fire department, building code administrator, or local agricultural college extension service.

USING EXISTING CHIMNEYS

Q. Can I hook my wood stove to the same chimney that my existing furnace uses?

A. Preferably not. Many building ordinances around the country still allow this practice, but some are changing. A stove may be operated safely on a proper Class A or masonry flue along with other appliances. However, the system would take much more inspection and maintenance, and the chance of having problems does increase.

Oil furnaces use barometric dampers, and most gas furnaces use a vent or hood to allow excess air into the chimney and to moderate draft in the chimney. These devices will function when the woodburner is operating and can cause the same excess airflow to the chimney. For most wood stoves, this is unnecessary and undesirable. The excess air cools the stack, thereby causing greater creosote buildup potential. If a chimney fire were to start, the barometric damper or gas hood would allow too much air to the creosote fire and it would more likely burn out of control.

Some people suggest that smoke, ashes, and sparks may backflow between two units on the same stack. This is possible, but not probable. If you have a large, sound existing Class A chimney, and must use this chimney for your wood stove, the woodburner should be connected 12" to 18" below the conventional furnace. When hookups of this kind are used, weekly or bimonthly inspections of the chimney should be made to make sure the system is staying clean. Then clean when ¼" creosote builds up.

It is always best, if you have the choice, to use only one heat-producing appliance per chimney. A good airtight woodburner deserves its own chimney.

CHOOSING WOOD STOVES

Q. What is the "best" type of stove to use as a freestanding supplementary heater?

A. The "best" stove depends upon a home's layout, where the stove is to be placed, where people spend most of their time while at home, and the amount of a home's heating load that the homeowner intends for the wood stove to assume. You have two basic choices to make when considering an airtight freestanding stove. This choice is between a radiant and a circulating type of stove.

It's important to first understand the difference between a radiant stove and a circulator. A radiant stove is the traditional stove design; nothing more than a cast-iron or sheet steel device that transmits most of its heat to the home by direct radiation. This means that walls, furniture, objects in the room, and people absorb the energy directly. There is very little warming of the air in the room where the stove is placed, and other rooms and spaces far away from the stove do not get as warm as the room where the stove is located.

Radiant stoves can be a disadvantage for the homeowner who wishes to have wood heat all parts of the house, but a real advantage to someone who wants the ultimate in comfortable single-room or open-space heating. Radiant heating stoves are the best choice if you plan to spend a great deal of time in the room where the stove is placed.

Circulating stoves, as their name implies, are capable of circulating heat to other parts of the house. The bulk of the heat they provide for the house is in warmed air. Through natural convection or forced-air fans, this warmed air can be moved around the house or ducted into existing heat-distribution systems. These stoves, while not as quaint or attractive in appearance as radiant stoves, are the best choice for those who desire maximum heat distribution to all parts of the house, and for those who wish to place the stove in a basement area or other location away from where the family spends its time.

Another important consideration is that radiant stoves have hot surfaces and circulators have warm surfaces. This may have a bearing where small children are present, or limited space between the stove and combustibles is available. The circulator can be placed closer to walls and other combustibles and will not be as hot to the touch as radiants.

FEEDING WOOD STOVES

Q. How long will a typical stove hold fire after loading?

A. This depends on many variables. Many stoves, especially non-grated base burners, can have glowing coals in them several days after loading. The size and style of the stove, the kind of woodburner, the mixture content of the wood, the size and layout of the area to be heated, the quality of insulation and weatherstripping, and the weather outside are all variables. This is why most stove maker claims of the number of square feet that a particular model will heat are rather ludicrous.

An important key is the heat load of the area you desire to heat. An average 1,500-square-foot home, with average insulation and one exchange of infiltration air per hour, will need an average of 20,000 to 30,000 Btu's per hour during the heating season in northern climates. If 25,000 Btu's are assumed as a basic requirement, here is some math that can show how long the fire can heat a home:

If the stove will hold 60 pounds of red oak per fill, and the wood is air dried to about 20% moisture content, the total potential energy load in the stove will be 384,000 Btu's (6,400 Btu's per pound of available energy x 60 pounds = 384,000 Btu's). If you assume that the stove has an efficiency ratio of about 55% (which is as good or better than most), that will mean we can expect an actual 211,200 Btu's out of that load to get into the home. Accordingly, you could expect that stove to heat the home for a period of about 8½ hours. (211,200 Btu's ÷ 25,000 Btu's per hour load = 8.448). In this hypothetical case, the stove would be out after 8½ hours. In actuality, the stove will not produce exactly 25,000 Btu's per hour, but would show a slightly higher rate in the first half of the burn and a tapering-off rate beyond the 8½ hours in the second half.

Also, if the weather were terribly cold and windy, the heat load for the same home could go as high as 40,000 to 50,000 Btu's per hour. If that were the case, to meet the needs of the home, the stove would have to be burned harder. Usually efficiency decreases in these high-power burns. Here's a look at burning times under these conditions:

> 60-pound load, 20% moisture red oak = 384,000 Btu's.
> Heat load of home = 50,000 Btu's/hr.
> Stove efficiency decreased to 50%.
> Total Btu's available to home = 384,000 x .5 = 192,000 Btu's.
> 192,000 ÷ 50,000 = 3.84 hours per load.

As you can see, the stove will function within its own limitations, and be affected by external conditions. The same stove, in two different installations with differing heat loads and weatherproofing, will function as differently as if it were two different brands.

SELECTING WOOD

Q. What are the best woods to burn?

A. It depends upon where you live. In general, the best firewood is the densest hardwood available to you in your area. However, in some areas dense hardwoods are much more expensive and hard to get. In this case, the best woods are those that are most cost-effective to burn. For example, if you lived in northern Michigan, had aspen growing in your backyard, and would have to haul red oak for 100 miles to get it home, you would be better off using the aspen, even if it was only 60% as good a fuel as red oak.

By the same token, if you were buying wood and could get red oak for $60 per cord and aspen for $45, you would be much better off buying the oak. In other words, it would take $74 worth of aspen at $45/cord to give you the same amount of energy available in one cord of red oak at $60/cord. No matter what wood you use, make sure it is dry (seasoned to 20% moisture content). This takes at least nine months or more in most climates after cutting, splitting, and stacking.

WOOD HEAT VALUE

Q. Do different woods have differing heat values?

A. By the cord or volume measure, yes. By the pound, no. According to studies done by the Forest Products Laboratory, U.S. Forest Service, there is little difference in Btu value/pound between woods, assuming moisture contents are the same. Softwoods may show slightly higher values because of their high resin content, but the difference is insignificant. By volume, there are obvious differences, as mentioned in the preceding answer.

STOVES AND WALLS

Q. How close can I put my stove to a combustible wall?

A. The distance from combustible surfaces that you place stoves, heaters, or furnaces is very important. NFPA recommendations (shown on page 133) are very strong and time tested. Follow them. They give the suggested clearances and tolerances for various stove types, along with shielding alternatives. If you choose not to use these recommendations, make allowances by over-spacing or over-shielding. Don't take chances.

VALUE OF HEAT EXCHANGERS

Q. Do stack heat exchangers really work as well as some manufacturers claim?

A. If you burned only very dry wood in open-front or leaky stoves, and operated them at high heat output all of the time, a stack heat exchanger would be a good device to use. If you have a good airtight stove and operate it for long-duration burns, leave the stack heat exchangers alone. They could cause you more problems than they are worth. In airtight systems they can cool the stack to produce excessive creosote deposits, and can impede draft.

USING STOVEPIPE

Q. How much stovepipe should one use in hooking a stove to a chimney? Doesn't the stovepipe help heat the house?

A. The current NFPA recommendation is that the stovepipe length should be no more than 75% of the height of the chimney between the point of stovepipe connections and the top. Safety should take precedence. Keep the stovepipe connector as short as possible—6' to 8' is long enough. Stovepipe will act as a further radiant surface to transfer heat to the home. But long sections will over-cool the stack, and have a tendency to plug up with creosote.

COMBUSTION AIR

Q. Should outside air be supplied to woodburning appliances such as wood stoves, furnaces, and fireplaces?

A. This seemingly simple question has many interesting ramifications. All combustion appliances need sufficient air to burn properly. Modern, tightly constructed homes have low infiltration rates, and an outside supply of make-up air may be necessary to run conventional furnaces as well as woodburning systems. Outside air need not be brought directly to an appliance, however. Where forced-air central heating systems are used, a properly sized outside air duct to the cold-air return on the furnace may be sufficient to supply combustion air for all wood stoves, furnaces, and fireplaces operating in the home. For stoves or furnaces, a 5" or 6" duct through the outside wall and into the stove or furnace room may be sufficient. Cold air ducted directly into the fireplace may be advantageous, but cold air may be better used if brought to the general area of the fireplace. In any case, outside air ducts should have dampers in them so that they can be controlled or shut off completely if necessary.

Ducting outside air directly into a burning chamber can be counterproductive. Cold outside temperatures can reduce firebox temperatures and reduce combustion efficiency. Excessive cooling of the stack and greater creosote formation can also result. The primary need for outside air in tightly constructed homes is not as much for increased efficiency as it is for the reduction of negative pressure.

In conventional or loosely constructed older homes, outside air is not as necessary to proper combustion, because the infiltration rate provides plenty of air.

Airtight stoves and furnaces will operate better with inside air, however. They don't remove that much air anyway when they operate at low-level burns. If fireplaces have no glass door closures, the home may benefit from outside air sources near the fireplace. Drafts in the home will be reduced, and infiltration rates will be reduced. If glass doors are used in closed position, the value of outside air induction into the home is diminished. The most important consideration is that sufficient air is needed for combustion, whether it comes from natural infiltration or from special ducts. Outside air ducts should be easily regulated with conveniently located dampers.

SMOKING STOVES

Q. How does one stop a stove from smoking?

A. This is another complicated problem. Some stoves are inherent smokers because of their design. Their flue openings are too small and their door openings are too large. Usually smoking is caused by one or more of the following factors:

■Chimney flue too small or large.

■Chimney too short.

■Chimney plugged up.

■Stovepipe has too many elbows. (No more than two 90° elbows should be used.)

■Stovepipe runs too long.

■Stack heat reclaimers are being used.

■Negative air pressure in the home. (There is not enough air for combustion; or other appliances such as dryers, furnaces, exhaust fans, etc. working while the stove is used are causing smoke to be pulled out of the stove into the home.)

■External obstructions. (Tall trees, buildings, landforms, etc. near the chimney can cause unusual draft patterns and downdrafts.)

■Weather conditions. (Many systems draft poorly on low-pressure foul-weather days, but may function nicely during high-pressure periods. When outside temperatures warm up, some systems don't operate as well as when it is cold.)

■Chimney caps being used. (These sometimes inhibit draft.)

■Poor wood. (Wet or punky wood does not burn as well. Lower stack temperatures result in poor draft and more smoking.)

■Poorly insulated chimney. (Air-cooled or exposed masonry chimneys sometimes smoke more. Chimneys constructed inside the home usually work better.)

STOVE INSTALLATION

Q. What are things a homeowner should check when installing a wood stove?

A. The following list, compiled by extension agricultural engineers at Cornell University, is a good one to follow as a guide to installing any woodburning device. If you follow the suggestions, problems should be kept to a minimum.

Before starting the first fire in your stove use this checklist to be sure that it is safely installed.

_____ 1. The stove does not have broken parts or large cracks that make it unsafe to operate.

_____ 2. A layer of sand or brick has been placed in the bottom of the firebox if suggested by the stove manufacturer.

_____ 3. The stove is located on a noncombustible floor, or an approved floor protection material is placed under the stove.

_____ 4. Floor protection extends out 6" to 12" from the sides and back of the stove and 18" from the front where the wood is loaded.

_____ 5. The stove is spaced at least 36" away from combustible material. If not, fire-resistant materials are used to protect woodwork and other combustible materials.

_____ 6. Stovepipe of 22- or 24-gauge metal is used.

_____ 7. The stovepipe diameter is not reduced between the stove and the chimney flue.

_____ 8. A damper is installed in the stovepipe near the stove unless one is built into the stove.

_____ 9. The total length of stovepipe is less than 10'.

_____ 10. There are at least 18" between the top of the stovepipe and the ceiling or other combustible material.

_____ 11. The stovepipe slopes upward toward the chimney and enters the chimney higher than the outlet of the stove firebox.

_____ 12. The stovepipe enters the chimney horizontally through a fire clay thimble that is higher than the outlet of the stove firebox.

_____ 13. The stovepipe does not extend into the chimney flue lining.

_____ 14. The inside thimble diameter is the same size as the stovepipe for a snug fit.

_____ 15. A double-walled ventilated metal thimble is used where the stovepipe goes through an interior wall.

_____ 16. The stovepipe does not pass through a floor, closet, or concealed space, or enter the chimney in the attic.

_____ 17. An UL-approved ALL FUEL metal chimney is used where a masonry chimney is not available or practical.

_____ 18. The chimney is in good repair.

_____ 19. The chimney flue lining is not blocked.

_____ 20. The chimney flue lining and the stovepipe are clean.

_____ 21. A metal container with tight-fitting lid is available for ash disposal.

_____ 22. The building official or fire inspector has approved the installation.

_____ 23. The company insuring the building has been notified of the installation.

11

Wood-Heating References

GLOSSARY

Air Intake. Source of combustion air feeding a woodburning unit. If unit has two systems for delivering air, main source is primary air intake. Air from second source supports burning as needed, and is drawn through secondary air intake.

Airtight Stove. Stove with all seams filled and a very tight door. No air can enter stove except at draft control. Gives operator full control over burning rate.

Bimetal Thermostat. Sensitive metal-coil thermostat used to automatically regulate the flow of air over wood fire, keeping room temperature at desired setting.

Box Stove. Four-legged, rectangular- or oval-shaped stove with draft at one end. Generally not convertible to a fireplace.

Btu (British Thermal Unit). The amount of heat required to raise the temperature of one pound of water one degree Fahrenheit.

Baffle Plate. Metal plate that holds hot gases and heated air in stove longer, causing them to travel a longer path before exiting; brings and holds them in close contact with the stove plates. This can result in more heat from the same amount of fuel.

Charcoal. Wood after all volatile substances have been heated and driven off. Consists mainly of carbon and gives intense, efficient heat.

Chimney. Upright tube for conducting smoke and gases from house. Can be heavy masonry or a pipe consisting of two or more layers of steel which are separated by insulation.

Condensate. Liquid resulting when water in vapor form contacts cool surface.

Convection. Heat transfer by warmed room air moving by gravity to other parts of house. One method by which a stove heats your home.

Cord. Stack of wood that is 4' wide by 4' high by 8' long and contains a gross space of 128 cubic feet.

Creosote. Black tarlike substance which is deposited on the inside of stoves, smoke pipe, and chimneys.

Cubic. Measure of volume that is calculated by multiplying width times length times height.

Damper. Flat round plate located inside pipe collar or smoke pipe, used to change the strength of the chimney draft.

Draft Control. Any device used to change amount of combustion air admitted to firebox. Sometimes called a draft regulator.

Efficiency. Quality of producing maximum heat with least wood.

Front-End Combustion. Combustion air enters stove at front and burns wood from front to back.

Face Cord. Wood cut 12", 16", or 24" long and stacked 4' high and 9' long. Don't confuse with a cord.

Green Wood. Wood that is still standing or just freshly cut and has the highest moisture content. Don't confuse with wet wood.

Heat Exchanger. Arched chamber added to a box stove to

increase efficiency. Also, device to salvage heat from fireplace fires via hollow tubes, or device to "scrub" heat from smoke passing through chimney.

Radiation. Heat transfer from a stove directly to another surface such as a wall, furniture, or you without affecting the temperature in between.

Refractory. Ground-up asbestos substance mixed with concrete and applied to the bottom of a firebox to provide added protection against burnout.

Roof Pitch. Measure of steepness of a roof expressed as number of inches roof rises for each foot of horizontal run.

Smoke Pipe. Stovepipe. Single wall pipe venting stove to chimney.

Stove Rake. Tool shaped like a hoe and used to manage ashes and embers in a wood stove.

AGENCIES AND ASSOCIATIONS

Following is a partial listing of further sources of information on heating with wood.

Chimney Sweep Association, Kristia Associates, P.O. Box 1176, Portland, Me. 04104

Energy Institute, Box 1, Fiddlers Green, Waitsfield, Vt. 05673

The Fireplace Institute, 111 E. Wacker Dr., Chicago, Ill. 60601

National Bureau of Standards, Washington, D.C. 20234

National Fire Protection Association, 470 Atlantic Ave., Boston, Mass. 02210

U.S. Dept. of Agriculture, Washington, D.C. 20250

U.S. Forest Service, Dept. of Agriculture, South Building, 12th and Independence Ave. S.W., Washington, D.C. 20036

Wood Energy Institute, Box 1, Fiddlers Green, Waitsfield, Vt. 05673

Departments of Natural Resources

Following is a state-by-state listing.

Alabama

Dept. of Conservation
  and Natural Resources
Administration Building
Montgomery 36104

Alaska

Dept. of Natural Resources
Pouch M
Juneau 99801

Arizona

Land Dept.
1624 W. Adams St.
Phoenix 85007

Arkansas

Geological Commission
3819 W. Roosevelt Rd.
Little Rock 72204

California

Dept. of Conservation
1416 9th St.
Sacramento 95814

Colorado

Dept. of Natural Resources
1845 Sherman
Denver 80203

Connecticut

Dept. of Environmental Protection
State Capitol
Hartford 06115

Delaware

Dept. of Natural Resources
  and Environmental Control
Tatnall Building
Dover 19901

Florida

Dept. of Natural Resources
Crown Building
Tallahassee 32304

Georgia

Dept. of Natural Resources
270 Washington St. SW
Atlanta 30334

Hawaii

Dept. of Land & Natural Resources
State Office Building
Honolulu 96809

Idaho

Dept. of Water Resources
4th and Fort Sts.
Boise 83720

Illinois

Dept. of Conservation
602 State Office Building
Springfield 62706

Indiana

Dept. of Natural Resources
State Office Building
Indianapolis 46204

Iowa

Natural Resources Council
Grimes Building
Des Moines 50319

Kentucky

Dept. of Natural Resources
  and Environmental Protection
Capital Plaza Tower
Frankfort 40601

Louisiana

Dept. of Conservation
Land and Natural Resources
    Building
Baton Rouge 70804

Maine

Dept. of Conservation
State Office Building
Augusta 04330

Maryland

Dept. of Natural Resources
Tawes State Office Building
Annapolis 21401

Massachusetts

Dept. of Natural Resources
State Office Building
Boston 02202

Michigan

Dept. of Natural Resources
Steven T. Mason Building
Lansing 48926

Minnesota

Dept. of Natural Resources
Centennial Building
St. Paul 55155

Missouri

Dept. of Natural Resources
Box 176
Jefferson City 65101

Montana

Dept. of Natural Resources
    and Conservation
32 S. Ewing St.
Helena 59601

Nebraska

Natural Resources Commission
Terminal Building
Lincoln 68508

Nevada

Dept. of Conservation
    and Natural Resources
213 Nye Building
Carson City 89701

New Hampshire

Dept. of Resources
    and Economic Development
State House Annex
Concord 03301

New Jersey

Dept. of Environmental
    Protection
John Fitch Plaza
Trenton 08625

New Mexico

Natural Resources Conservation
    Commission
321 W. San Francisco
Santa Fe 87501

New York

Dept. of Environmental
    Conservation
50 Wolf Rd.
Albany 12205

North Carolina

Dept. of Natural and Economic
    Resources
Administration Building
Raleigh 27611

North Dakota

Natural Resources Council
State Capitol
Bismarck 58505

Ohio

Dept. of Natural Resources
Fountain Square
Columbus 43224

Oregon

Natural Resources
207 State Capitol
Salem 97310

Pennsylvania

Dept. of Environmental Resources
202 Evangelical Press Building
Harrisburg 17105

Rhode Island

Dept. of Natural Resources
83 Park St.
Providence 02903

South Carolina

Development Board
1301 Gervais St.
Columbia 29201

South Dakota

Dept. of Natural Resources Development
State Office Building #2
Pierre 57501

Tennessee

Dept. of Conservation
2611 W. End Ave.
Nashville 37203

Utah

Dept. of Natural Resources
438 State Capitol
Salt Lake City 84114

Vermont

Natural Resources Conservation
Council
Environmental Conservation
Agency
5 Court St.
Montpelier 05602

Virginia

Dept. of Conservation
and Economic Development
1100 State Office Building
Richmond 23219

Washington

Dept. of Natural Resources
Public Lands Building
Olympia 98504

West Virginia

Dept. of Natural Resources
State Office Building #3
Charleston 25305

Wisconsin

Dept. of Natural Resources
4610 University Ave.
Madison 53701

WOODBURNING STOVES

Below is a partial listing of manufacturers of woodburning stoves and related equipment.

Abundant Life Farm, P.O. Box 63, Lochmere, N.H. 03252; *All Nighter Stove Works*, 80 Commerce St., Glastonbury, Conn. 06033; *Ashley*, Div. of Martin Industries, P.O. Box 128, Florence, Ala. 35630; *Atlanta Stove Works, Inc.*, Atlanta, Ga. 30307; *Autocrat Corp.*, New Athens, Ill. 62264; *Birmingham Stove and Range Co.*, P.O. Box 2647, Birmingham, Ala. 35202; *Borneo Sumatra Trading Co.*, 75 Union Ave., Rutherford, N.J. 07070; *Bow & Arrow Imports*, 14 Arrow St., Cambridge, Mass. 02138; *C & H Manufacturing*, 654 N. Colony Rd., Wallingford, Conn. 06492; *Cawley/Le-May Stove Co.*, Box 431, RD 1, Barto, Pa. 19504; *Empire Stove Co.*, Belleville, Ill. 62222; *Fatsco*, 251 Fair Ave., Benton Harbor, Mich. 49022; *Fire-View Distributors*, P.O. Box 370, Rogue River, Ore. 97537; *Fisher Stoves*, River Rd., Rt. 3, Bow, N.H. 03301; *Free Flow Stove Works*, Mine Rd., South Strafford, Vt. 05070; *Gibraltar Stoves*, Div. of RA-MAC Welding, 112 Osborne Rd., Fridley, Minn. 55432; *Hearth Craft*, 10035 N.E. Sandy Blvd., P.O. Box 20584, Portland, Ore. 97220; *Hydraform Products Corp.*, Box 2409, Rochester, N.H. 03867; *KNT*, Box 25, Hayesville, Ohio 44838; *Kickapoo Stove Works, Ltd.*, Box 127-56, La Farge, Wis. 54639; *Kristia Associates*, 343 Forest Ave., P.O. Box 1118, Portland, Maine 04104; *Locke Stove Co.*, 114 W. 11th St., Kansas City, Mo. 64105; *Lyons Supply Co.*, 1 Perimeter Rd., Manchester, N.H. 03108; *Metal Building Products, Inc.*, Nashua, N.H. 03060; *Mohawk Industries*, P.O. Box 71-1, Adams, Mass. 01220; *Monarch, Malleable Iron Range Co.*, Beaver Dam, Wis. 53916; *New Hampshire Wood Stoves*, Fairgrounds Rd., Plymouth, N.H. 03264; *Pioneer Lamps & Stoves*, 71 Yesler Way, Seattle, Wash. 98104; *Pipe Products Co.*, 1274 Lincoln Rd., Allegan, Mich. 49010; *Ram Forge*, Brooks, Maine 04921; *Riteway Manufacturing Co.*, Box 6, Harrisonburg, Va. 22801; *Scandinavian Stoves, Inc.*, Box 72, Alstead, N.H. 03602; *Self Sufficiency Products*, One Appletree Square,

Minneapolis, Minn. 55420; *Sevca*, Box 396, Bellows Falls,
Vt. 05101; *Shenandoah Manufacturing Co., Inc.*, P.O. Box
839, Harrisonburg, Va. 22801; *Shrader Wood Stoves*, 4425
Main St., Springfield, Ore. 97477; *Southport Stoves*, 248
Tolland St., East Hartford, Conn. 06108; *Stove Works*, P.O.
Box 172A, Marlboro, Vt. 05344; *Suburban*, P.O. Box 399,
Dayton, Tenn. 37321; *Thermo-Control Wood Stoves*, Coble-
skill, N.Y. 12043; *Thulman Eastern Corp.*, 3485 Chevrolet
Dr., Ellicott City, Md. 21043; *Timberline Stoves, Ltd.*, 1840
LeMoyne Ave., Syracuse, N.Y. 13208; *Torrid Manufacturing
Co., Inc.*, 1248 Poplar Pl. So., Seattle, Wash. 98144; *United
States Stove Co.*, South Pittsburgh, Tenn. 37380; *Vermont
Castings, Inc.*, Box 126, Randolph, Vt. 05060; *Vermont Wood
Stove Co.*, P.O. Box 1016, Bennington, Vt. 05201; *Warmglow
Products, Inc.*, 625 Century S.W., Grand Rapids, Minn.
49503; *Washington Stove Works*, P.O. Box 687, Everett,
Wash. 98201; *Whittier Steel & Manufacturing*, 10725 S.
Painter Ave., Sante Fe Springs, Calif. 90670; *Woodland
Stove Co.*, 6½ S. Fredrick, Oelwein, Iowa 50662.

PREFAB FIREPLACES & FIREPLACE EQUIPMENT

Below is a partial listing of companies that offer prefab
fireplaces and fireplace equipment.

Bassani Manufacturing, 3726 E. Miraloma, Anaheim,
Calif. 92806; *General Products*, 150 Ardale St., West Haven,
Conn. 06516; *Heatilator*, Mt. Pleasant, Iowa 52641; *Heritage
Fireplace Equipment*, 1874 Englewood Ave., Akron, Ohio
44312; *Isothermics*, Box 86, Augusta, N.J. 07882; *LaFont
Corp.*, 1319 Town St., Prentice, Wis. 54556; *Majestic*, Hunt-
ington, Ind. 46750; *Malm Fireplaces, Inc.*, 368 Yolanda Ave.,
Santa Rosa, Calif. 95404; *Martin Industries*, P.O. Box 1527,
Huntsville, Ala. 35807; *Nas-Corp.*, 230 Fifth Ave., Suite
1702, New York, N.Y. 10001; *Preway*, Wisconsin Rapids,
Wis. 54494; *Richardson's Fireplaces*, 2031 Hillcrest Lane,
Burley, Idaho 83318; *Ridgway Steel Fabricators*, Ridgway,
Pa. 15853; *Superior Fireplace Co.*, 4325 Artesia Ave., Fuller-
ton, Calif. 92633; *Temtex Products*, P.O. Box 1184, Nash-
ville, Tenn. 37202; *Thermalite Corp.*, P.O. Box 658, Brent-

wood, Tenn. 37027; *Thermograte*, 2875 Fairview Ave., St. Paul, Minn. 55113.

MULTI-FUEL FURNACES

Following is a partial listing of companies that make wood-burning furnaces.

Arotek Corp., 1703 East Main St., Torrington, Conn. 06790; *Bellway Manufacturing*, Grafton, Vt. 05146; *Charmaster Products*, 2307 Hwy. 2 West, Grand Rapids, Minn. 55744; *Combo Furnace Co.*, 1707 W. 4th St., Grand Rapids, Minn. 55744; *Duo-Matic*, 2413 Bond St., Park Forest So., Ill. 60466; *Integrated Thermal Systems*, 379 State St., Portsmouth, N.H. 03801; *Longwood Furnace Corp.*, Gallatin, Mo. 64640; *Marathon Heater Co.*, Box 265, RD 2, Marathon, N.Y. 13803; *Oneida Heater Co.*, Box 148, Oneida, N.Y. 13421; *Riteway Manufacturing Co.*, Box 6, Harrisonburg, Va. 22801; *Wilson Industries*, 2296 Wycliff St., St. Paul, Minn. 55114.

HELPER UNITS

Below is a partial listing of manufacturers that offer units to connect into existing fossil-fuel furnaces.

American Way, 190 Range Rd., Wilton, Conn. 06897; *Arrowsmith Industries, Inc.*, Box 208, Dowington, Pa. 19335; *Bellway Manufacturing Co.*, Grafton, Vt. 05146; *C & D Distributors, Inc.*, P.O. Box 766, Old Saybrook, Conn. 06475; *Combo Furnace Co.*, 1707 W. 4th St., Grand Rapids, Minn. 55744; *Daka Corp.*, 5335 N. County Rd. 18, Minneapolis, Minn. 55428; *Duo-Matic of Canada*, Box 610, Waterford, Ontario, Canada; *Energy-Mate, Inc.*, 1415 Lynn Ave., Altonna, Wis. 54720; *General Products Corp.*, 20 Railroad Ave., West Haven, Conn. 06516; *Gibraltar*, Div. of Ramac Welding, 112 Osborne Rd., Fridley, Minn. 55432; *Heat-N-Glo*, 1100 Riverwood Dr., Burnsville, Minn. 55337; *Itasca Manufacturing, Inc.*, P.O. Box 105, Menahga, Minn. 56464; *Johnson Energy Systems*, 7350 N. 76th St., Milwaukee, Wis. 53223; *Len-Jay Furnace Co.*, Underwood, Minn. 56586; *Marathon Heater Co.*, Box 165, Marathon, N.Y. 13803; *Minne-*

sota *Energy Savers, Inc.,* 305 Main, La Crescent, Minn. 55947; *Preston Distributing Co.,* 11 Whidden St., Lowell, Mass. 01852; *Monarch, Malleable Iron Range Co.,* Beaver Dam, Wis. 53916; *Riteway Manufacturing Co.,* P.O. Box 6, Harrisonburg, Va. 22801; *Silver Star Corp.,* 5765 Wildlife Dr., Allentown, Wis. 53002; *Thermo-Control,* Cobleskill, N.Y. 12043; *United States Stove Co.,* South Pittsburgh, Tenn. 37380; *Vermont Woodstove Co.,* P.O. Box 1016-011, Bennington, Vt. 05201; *Wilson Industries,* 2296 Wycliff, St. Paul, Minn. 55114.